THE POWER
of
SELF TALK

Empower Positive Thinking, Create a Positive Aura and
Redesign Your Personal, Professional and Spiritual Life

BHAVYA MANGLA

Published by
Bhavya Mangla
(bhavyamangla@gmail.com)

To
my family and my teachers

Contents

Preface

When I decided to write a book, there were many thoughts which were crossing my mind. I was trying to figure out the most important and relevant subject for me. While going through this process, I realized that Self-Talk is something which has remained with me for many years. I have experienced the worst and good side of it in myself. In my teenage, unintended but constant negative self-talk was responsible for my low self-esteem. It continued till the age of 30 years when I first realized the futility of my negative self-expression. But since then, it has been a roller-coaster ride for me. I have seen drastic transformation inside myself and it is continuing so far. The single most important factor for this transformation is understanding of *my* self-talk and its impact on my sub-conscious mind.

I concluded that this is a subject which touch everyone's life in many ways. Knowingly and unknowingly, we are consistently talking negative and still expecting good results in our internal and external world. We may be successful in the external world but at what cost and suffering? While writing about Self-Talk, I found that I am connecting with all relevant topics like conscious and subconscious mind, positivity, power of thinking positively, how to think correctly, power of now and many more.

I always wanted to express myself in words but was not sure whether I can do it and when should I do it. I was also not certain whether I will be able to write so many words! But when I started writing, I could find that there is a plethora of ideas and examples which were waiting to come out. After I completed my first draft, I realized that I have written much more than what I had anticipated in the beginning. The simple thumb rule that I followed was to write at least 600 words every day. The only challenge that I faced after completing the first draft was that I had penned many short stories/experiences of 600 words! It took some time to link them together as one book. To any first-time writer, the biggest challenge is to keep consistency and momentum.

The biggest benefit that I have got after writing this book is that I have become much more aware of my thoughts, got much more conscious about what I am feeding myself and have become much more responsible for myself.

Bhavya Mangla

Acknowledgements

As I look exactly 12 months back, I was not having an iota of an idea that I will be completing my first book within the next year. Although, it was always in the bucket list that someday I will write when I was not sure. The seed of writing book germinated from my father Dr NK Mangla, who has written many books related to Yoga, English language and textbooks for school (Commerce, Accountancy, Business Studies & Economics). Today I feel that my father would have been very proud of my first achievement.

In April 2019, my mentor, Vidyanand, prompted me to write a book about my experiences so far. He gave me the confidence that I can express myself in words. When I initiated the process, another noble soul, Som Bathla, helped regarding how to write a book, structure it, its different steps & possible challenges. Hasnain Waris was another good friend who helped me on the entire journey. Deeptendu Ahuja helped in editing the updated version.

While writing, there were many sources of inspiration including Toastmasters International which instigated the creativity in me and spiritual guidance by Sister Shivani of Brahma Kumaris.

This book is vastly influenced by my personal experiences, practical experiments, many erudite writers like Shad Helmstetter, Joseph Murphy, Brian Tracy and above all the holy book, the Gita.

The support of the family was immense who backed me for everything. My mother, Bina Mangla, always gave me confidence that whatever I am doing is good, my wife, Rekha, who went out of the way to make me feel comfortable so that I can write peacefully, my elder brother Divya, my younger son, Lagan, who read my first draft and guided me in many areas for improvement, my elder son, Utsav, who supported me on technical matters and my friend, Vinay, who has always supported me for many years.

CHAPTER

1

Introduction

Why you are Reading this Book?

As this book is in your hand and you are reading it, it means

- You are genuinely interested in improving your quality of life

- You care about your present and future

- You are conscious of the present

- You are committed to your wellbeing

- You are looking for a change

- You think that self-talk has a very important role in life

- You believe in the power of the subconscious mind

- You want to understand the difference between the conscious and subconscious mind

Your Expectations

In this fast-paced life, when you decide to invest your time and money for something new, you always have great expectations. The flow of information is so huge that it is difficult to sustain your attention on one thing. The theory of multi-tasking (*although flawed*) has been ingrained in our mindset such that even while reading this book, you may be checking updates on social media, maybe watching something on Netflix, or you may be having a hot cup of coffee or tea, with soothing or loud music playing in the background. You may be surrounded by friends while trying to concentrate on this book, you may be travelling and having dinner, and so many more possible things. Under these circumstances, this book needs to capture your attention so you can forget about the distractions around you. It should give you something to intake regularly in your day-to-day life.

The language of the book should be so easy that you need not refer to a dictionary. (*Hey, when was the last time you referred to it!*) The book should be structured in a reader-friendly way so you can understand the flow. Different topics should be aligned so that transitions are smooth. The content should be easy to understand lest you go back to social media. (*Sometimes you do not know why. Maybe it's an addiction!*) The book should give you something you can implement in your fast-paced life without much effort. It should strike a chord within you. It should remind you of the good values you learned in your childhood. It should strengthen your previous learning. The book should be a blueprint for your future, such that you feel proud of deciding to read it.

In short, it should be something about which you can

confidently tell your friends, colleagues or family members, I have invested my time in reading this book.

Who should Read this Book?

Over the last century, hundreds of books have been written on the 'Power of Self-Talk.' All of them have been extremely rich in their content and presentation. For decades, you have been reading these books and getting benefits. These books have helped you enhance knowledge and emotional quotient.

So, why another book? Maybe because you are looking for a book that:

♦ can connect *you* with *yourself*

♦ can be a mirror to know 'Who are you?'

♦ can answer at least some of your questions

♦ can be understood by people of all ages

♦ is easy in language

♦ is written from the perspective of the reader

♦ has relatable anecdotes and from day-to-day life

♦ and helps you to discover *yourself*

In the present times, with the explosion of information through digital platforms, it is challenging to find your way out of the maze and read/complete a book. You are constantly getting updated about any changes happening anywhere in the world. You always feel that you *know* everything. But too much information is also creating a vacuum. Is this you?

♦ Even though your mobile phone is charged, you still carry an additional power bank and charger.

♦ Your wallet has many credit and debit cards, but you are still searching for more money to safeguard your future.

♦ You have the best clothes and your closet is full, but you are still trying to show off how smart you look and want the approval of others.

♦ You are having a complete vanity kit but are still worried about your looks.

So, what to do? Should you continue your life like this, or can you *again* try to change something internally about yourself. This book is for people...

♦ Who are rich and famous but are still insecure about their position & wealth and looking for options to enjoy life better

♦ Who have succeeded in their professional lives but are struggling hard to keep their personal life intact

♦ Who are young and aiming very high but are afraid 'they might not achieve their goals'

♦ Who have lost hope of succeeding in life and are looking for a miracle

♦ Who has everything in life but are still not satisfied

♦ Who are successful professionals in their careers but are still insecure

♦ Who thought that when they become rich, they would be happy, but are still looking for it

◆ Who are in their teenage years with unbridled energy and want to channelize it in the right direction

◆ Who are afraid of public speaking but want to leave a mark on the world

◆ Who are busy professionals looking to strike a balance between their career, family life and health

◆ Who are looking for purpose and passion in life

◆ Who want mastery over their emotions

◆ Who are struggling to overcome procrastination, self-doubt, over-eating, smoking or any other habit

◆ Who wants more control over their choices every day

◆ Who want to have sound and blissful sleep

◆ Who want to have a better relationship with their parents, spouse, friends and colleagues

◆ Who want to bridge their Belief Gap (a gap between what you can achieve and what you think about yourself)

This book is for everyone who wants to live a peaceful, successful, healthier and enjoyable life.

What you can Learn

I don't think a book can make you learn anything. When you start reading to find out what you can learn (*it is not a textbook!*), it means you are already prejudiced, as you are searching for something (becoming judgmental) that you want to prove to yourselves. I think the best approach is to read this, or any book, to *just* read. While reading it organically, the book will engage you and align *you* with it. You will start talking to *yourself*. If this book can help you connect with *yourself*, it means it has been successful *for you*.

What you can Earn

These days, you do only those things from which you can *earn*. The respect of any family member varies according to how much the person is earning. The criteria of success for any individual is not the peace of mind and sound health but how much the person is earning. That is why we all are spending 12 to 16 hours every day to *earn,* although it is just *one* important aspect of our lives. By reading this book, you can earn

♦ better a relationship with yourself and others

♦ peace of mind

♦ the power of positive self-talk

♦ the most powerful ally i.e. your subconscious mind

♦ high quality of life and much more (*which may eventually lead to earning more money too!*)

In the end, we will review again, what have you learnt, earned and whether your expectations were met.

CHAPTER

2

Self-Talk

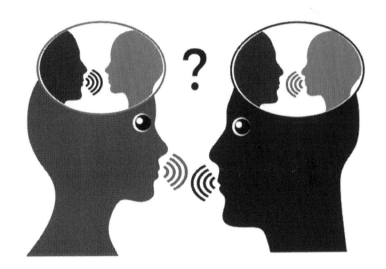

What is Self-Talk?

Self-Talk is an internal monologue or inner speech, i.e. a person's inner voice that provides a running commentary of conscious/unconscious thoughts.

According to a study, on average we have 45000 to 55000 thoughts in a day which translates into 25 to 35 thoughts a minute. It means that our mind keeps on fluctuating throughout the day. Like breathing, this is a normal process over which one does not seem to have any control. Consciously, a human being does not know whether or not it is breathing, still, we survive, even while sleeping! Similarly, thoughts keep on coming and going; and it looks like one has no control over it. In a research study, it has been concluded that thoughts cannot be controlled, but can very well be steered towards the direction of choice.

> *"No one can rest even for an instant without action. For one is always made to act by the forces born of nature"*
> —BHAGAVAD GITA VERSE 3.5

Self-Talk plays a dominant role in deciding how to direct your thoughts.

For example:

> *When you are in the office, do you need to force yourself to think about work-related matters?*
>
> *When you are with friends, do you force yourself to have thoughts related to them?*
>
> *When you are playing football, do you need to create thoughts related to the sport?*

The logical answer is NO. **But, when you want to pray to the almighty God, are you equally successful? Are you able to pray to god with the same focus and attention as you have, when with friends?**

For certain activities, you do not need to focus your attention but things still happen. On the other hand, while praying to God or studying a textbook, you have to *force* yourself! The reason for such a tendency is that wherever you are convinced, connected or have trust, you do not have to force yourself to focus your attention. Magic happens automatically!

Consider that you are in the office discussing a very important topic related to an upcoming board meeting but are facing regular distractions. You find that your colleague starts talking about an upcoming party tonight. You have two options, either to go ahead with the discussion about the party or politely tell your colleague that at this moment, the current topic is more important, and the party can wait. There is a possibility that your colleague may agree, but since the fever of the upcoming party is so high, he may intervene and again start discussing the agenda of tonight's party. Now you have a choice, either to get carried away with the colleague's discussion or stick to your work. This time, too, you politely but sternly tell your colleague to focus on the topic at hand which is more important and relevant at this moment, and to park discussion of the party (which may be important to you as well) done for a later time.

Something similar can be done while praying to God. There is a high probability that your attention will get diverted to your work, friends, children, social media, etc. You need to politely tell your unwanted thoughts to come knocking later. A similar thought can come back, this time more forcefully. But again, you need to politely but sternly tell your uninvited thought to wait 30 minutes. You can continue to do this process until your uninvited friend agrees to wait and you finish your prayer.

Self-Talk works wonders during such challenges. If you are consistently saying to yourself that YOU are stronger than *your* thoughts, YOU will certainly succeed. Constant self-talk will prime your subconscious mind, to achieve the desired result.

In the coming chapters, we will talk in detail about the power of self-talk and the subconscious mind.

My Experience with Self-Talk

"When your blood is circulating freely in your body, you are healthy. When money is circulating freely in your life, you are economically healthy. When people begin to hoard money, to put it away in tin boxes, and become charged with fear, there is an economic illness. When thoughts are flowing freely, you are healthy; when you stop, you become mentally ill."

—UNKNOWN

Knowingly, I have been doing self-talk since the year 2001. When I joined a multi-level marketing company, I got exposure to different types of books and audio cassettes wherein self-talk was given a lot of importance. I remember reading a book on self-talk by Dr Shad Helmstetter. Interestingly, while reading the book, I realized that I had been doing self-talk since my childhood, albeit unknowingly. Whenever I was in trouble or some pain, I prayed to God, "Let everything be ok." Whenever I was feeling afraid while travelling on a lonely road at night, the general communication in the family was that "talk positive, everything will be ok soon."

In your day-to-day life, you are doing self-talk without bothering about its content. At the end of the day, generally, you may be finding yourself exhausted. You might be wondering why you are feeling exhausted although you have not done any "heavy stuff." There is a popular saying, "Garbage in, garbage out." The root cause is that you are programming your mind throughout the day and are talking more negatively with yourself than positively.

While writing this book, I realized that since my early days, I was not only doing self-talk repeatedly for positive things but also negative things. One very common thought was related to "I am not good at doing this thing" or "I do not think I am looking attractive." I realized that these self-talks were very common in my day-to-day vocabulary. Unintentionally, I was praying to God to implement some bad things for me.

Over the years, I realized that Self-Talk is a powerful tool that creates an aura around us. If the aura is positive, you think you can do anything in the world. In the last 20 odd years, I have seen that I have been extremely successful in utilizing its power in both a positive and negative manner! The results have been enormously satisfying. I can vouch that there can be nothing stronger, powerful and more lethal than self-talk. It helps in changing the pattern from "impossible" to "I'm possible!"

While observing others, I have identified a certain pattern in their behaviour and success rate. I have seen many people always quibbling about something or other, and the result is that despite being in the best of situations, they are still not satisfied and are still craving for something else in life: in short, their life still looks unfulfilled. We must realize that we are the master of our destinies.

But why does it happen? Is it because we are not aware of its power or do not consider it important? I strongly think that this topic should be part of school and college curriculum. From early childhood, students should be made aware of the power of self-talk. If this habit is inculcated in them in early childhood, it will be of great service to the nation.

Conscious Mind

Your life is a reflection of your assumptions; believe you have received and you shall receive:

—UNKNOWN

We have two minds: Conscious and Subconscious. The conscious mind is the active mind that observes and does everything with attention. It has the power to make decision.

◆ Like this book in your hand. You are reading it in your conscious state.

◆ When you change the channels of your television using a remote, you are in a conscious state.

◆ When you are talking to others, *generally* you are in a conscious state.

◆ When you decided to buy this book, you must have been in your conscious state.

◆ When you are talking to your spouse, you are usually in a conscious state (or you will face immediate consequences, *consciously!*).

◆ When you type a message on WhatsApp, you are in a conscious state.

◆ After reading the above paragraph, when you are trying to find your present state of mind, it means you are in Conscious state.

Sub-conscious Mind

"The only path by which another person can upset you is through your own thought."

—JOSEPH MURPHY

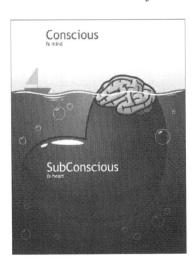

Our subconscious mind is subjective in nature. It does not decide or calculate anything. Whatever has been fed into it comes out as it is. Our subconscious mind is never willing to change and wants to do the things stored there by us.

Our subconscious mind has unlimited potential. Unlike financial banks, where you have a finite amount of money, your subconscious mind has infinite storage capacity. It stores everything irrespective of the quality of the content. Therefore, if you have the habit of waking up late in the morning, you'll find it difficult to change course and suddenly start waking up early.

Just like Google, where you write a query and retrieve information, your subconscious mind's function is to store everything and retrieve it when needed. Your job is to be aware of the program you are feeding into your subconscious mind.

The subconscious mind may be considered as a fertile land where your conscious mind bears fruits, vegetables, flowers, cacti, weeds, etc.

The subconscious mind never grows old. It is timeless, ageless, and endless. It is a part of the universal mind of God that was never born, and it will never die. Your subconscious never sleeps. It is always on the job. It controls all your vital functions.

A man on a horse came galloping quickly down the road. It appears the man had somewhere important to go. Another man, who was standing alongside the road, shouted, "Where are you going?" and the man on the horse replied, "I don't know! Ask the horse!"

—UNKNOWN

This is something happening to us 24x7. More than 80% of the time, we are working on autopilot mode. We do not know what we are doing, saying, writing or thinking, but we keep on doing it. It is a very interesting and courageous journey we all are going on, most of the time without realizing it. We think that everything is in *our* control, but we do not realize that it is not *we* but *our* subconscious mind that is in control of everything.

Our conscious mind has the power to choose a direction. Whatever is chosen goes to our subconscious mind which stores the information. Our conscious mind is the "watchman at the gate." Its chief function is to protect our subconscious mind from false impressions. If you choose to believe that something decent can happen, it will start happening. Our conscious mind *commands* and our subconscious mind *obeys*.

Say someone offers you a cigarette and you do not have a habit to smoke, the following things may happen:

(a) Your conscious mind will immediately come into action. What should I do?

(b) This information will go to your subconscious mind which has stored all your previous experience. The message may come that you do not smoke.

(c) Based on the feedback received from your subconscious mind and present knowledge of the conscious mind, you will decide to smoke or reject it.

Let us see a few examples related to Conscious & Subconscious Mind.

— While driving a car, do you apply the brakes with your left foot or right foot? As I write this, I am still not sure which foot *I use*, although I have been driving for the last 25 years.

— Do you notice while driving a car whether you are using both hands on the steering wheel or one (sometimes even none!). The reason is very simple: after a few years of driving, the entire process becomes so automatic that you do not realize how you are doing it. But, when you were learning, each movement counted. Your hands were always straight on the steering wheel. You were considering different steps in your mind; and certainly, there was no discussion and the music system was compulsorily off. You were using your conscious mind, which is always very active.

— When you are putting on trousers, have you ever thought which leg to insert first? Think it over. You would be amazed to note that irrespective of any situation, you will put your *right* leg in first! Am I right? Somewhere in your early childhood, you learned the art of putting your *right* leg in first and since then you continued to do it unconsciously. Now try to wear trousers today, consciously putting your *left* leg in first and enjoy the difference!

— While walking, have you ever tried to figure out which foot goes first (left or right)? At times, we run very fast and never try to find out how our legs are moving. Maybe if you tried too hard to discover it, you might fall in the process! Consider that when looking at your 10-month-old child, every footstep is measured. As parents, we always make sure that the child takes one step at a time. The first footstep is celebrated as a big occasion. Everything is done with full consciousness.

— How often has it happened that while eating food, instead of the spoon going to your mouth, it goes to your nose? No. Never. Why? Because you have tuned your mind such that even if you are eating in pitch dark, the spoon will always go in your mouth *only*. The mind is fully trained and functions in automatic mode. But have you ever noticed a one-year-old child learning how to eat custard? You will find custard everywhere except inside his or her mouth. Too much consciousness!

— When you are speaking in your native language, how often do you think before uttering any word? Never. Why? Because everything has been synchronized such that words come automatically when you speak out. (*Sometimes, you even surprise yourself when talking about something deep or cheap!*) I still remember the days when I was trying to learn the Russian language. Every word was coming out very slowly as if I was reading from somewhere and speaking out. My consciousness used to be so high that after speaking for some time, I realized that my jaw was aching!

— As I write these words on my laptop, how much attention am I paying to the keyboard? The simple answer is, not much. Why? Because I do not need to look at the keyboard. I am just looking at the screen and checking if the words are being typed correctly. But I can still recall my college days when I started practicing. I was using my index finger and searched for each word, always thinking it is easier to write on a piece of paper rather than punching on the keyboard. The attention level was very high.

— This morning when I went swimming, a childhood friend, who recently joined me asked me, "Can you help me learn to swim?" I said, yes, it is very easy. Just jump into the water and start rotating your shoulders and oscillate your feet—just swim. Then he asked me, how do you take a breath? I replied, periodically. I bring my head out and take a breath in and breath out in the water. I was finding it very difficult to communicate how I do it, as the entire process had become synchronous. Then I recalled the days, around 15 years back, when I had started learning swimming. It was a painful process. Hand and leg movements were counted. I could count every movement in my head, turning upward to take a breath. I was so alert and focused.

— A few weeks back, I was attending a conference. As a part of the dress code, we were supposed to wear a tie. Since my colleague was not used to wearing a tie, he came to my room and asked me how to knot a tie. I said, it's very simple and tried to explain it to him. It took me more than five times to teach him how to knot a tie. Why? Because it was so mechanical for me that I was finding it difficult to do it slowly and guide him. Have you ever tried teaching someone how to knot a tie? When you were learning, all your mental faculties were active and focused on the new art.

— You may have noticed that when you are watching a movie in a theatre and suddenly the power goes off, it becomes pitch dark. A few people in the audience will start whistling or shouting. Do they do it intentionally or does it just happen? They did not have an iota of an idea that the electricity was going to go off, but instantaneously, they *react*. The reason is that in their subconscious mind it is stored that whenever it becomes dark, they must shout or whistle.

If you look at the above situations, they have one thing in common: we have become so used to doing a particular activity that we cannot comprehend how it is happening. Things start happening flawlessly and it is challenging to find how. Our minds become so tuned to the work that we do not recall how it is functioning at the moment?

— Take another situation about drinking liquor. People start behaving differently than their normal selves. People will react differently to the same liquor. Some will become quiet, some violent, some speak more, some shout, some start dancing, some even weep. Why does the same liquor have a different impact on different people? *Is it that their real subconscious mind comes out?*

— When you are conscious, you control your behaviour; you manage what you say. You know how to respond/ react to any situation. You try to show your best to the world. But when you lose *your* consciousness and become partially unconscious, your *real* self comes out! Your true picture is in front of the world as you cannot fake it. Consciousness helps you to control things. But as you become unconscious of yourself, whatever is stored inside comes out without any pretension.

Can we conclude that our subconscious mind is extremely powerful? We just need to feed something into it, practice it every-day and it becomes part of us. We do not ever realize how strong it becomes part of our personality.

Vibrations

"If life throws you a few bad notes or vibrations, don't let them interrupt or alter your song"

—SUZY KASSEEM

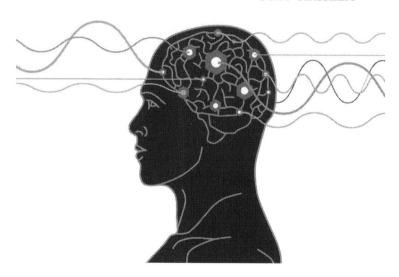

Vibration is an overall state of being. As per the first law of thermodynamics, energy can neither be created nor destroyed. It transforms itself from one form to another. As human beings, we are also experts in transmitting and transforming energy. We do it continually, knowingly or unknowingly. Everything in the universe is made up of energy vibrating at different frequencies. In the year 2000, I realized its power and started channelizing it in the right perspective. Since then, I have always found myself at a high frequency. People around me have also become used to it. Sometimes when my energy level is low, I am immediately questioned for it.

Energy, in the form of vibrations, plays a crucial role in our lives. At times, we don't understand its potency, but vibrations are always influencing our lives positively or negatively. For instance:

♦ When we are suffering from some fear

♦ When we are not satisfied with our performance

♦ When we are not able to execute our plans

♦ When we are in a habit of finding faults with everyone

♦ When we are on a high as we are going on date for the first time

One of the easiest ways to deal with any negative vibrations is to write down in detail what you are not able to achieve. When you write down your negative state of mind on paper, you are triggering your subconscious mind to identify/awaken deeply ingrained negative thoughts. As you continue with this process, everything immersed in your subconscious mind is reactivated. Once you burn that piece of paper, you burn the negative energy from your subconscious mind as well. As said earlier, energy can neither be created nor destroyed. You are converting one form of negative energy into another form.

You can question how the thoughts (negative in this case) sitting in our subconscious mind can be burned and transformed into another form (ash, fumes, etc.)? This seems to be a valid question and we must find out if there is an analogy to justify it.

On your birthday, assume your six-year-old child thinks of giving you a surprise and decides to make a birthday card. We all know the designing capability of a six-year kid in terms of quality, but we are all very sure that when the child hands over the surprise birthday card, emotions will be generated. It is obvious that when looking at the natural affection of a little child, you will be elated. Consider this: if that birthday card was for sale, how much money could be made? I am sure it is hardly any. But that birthday card will be precious and priceless to you for a very long time. Although the card hardly has any monetary value, it does generate a very high emotional energy quotient. Would you burn the card at any cost? The obvious answer is NO. Why? Because of the high emotional energy in that simple piece of paper.

Coming back to the earlier situation of the piece of paper onto which you are emoting your negative thoughts and beliefs. It has a high energy quotient, albeit negative. So, if you burn the paper full of negative thoughts, does it burn negative energy? The logical and obvious answer is Yes.

Vibrations are nothing but energy. Vibrations play a very important role in your life. You need to be extremely careful while generating them. Even if you have generated wrong thoughts, you know there is a way to manage them. Similarly, you also know how to channel positive energy to yourself. Self-Talk plays a very important role in channeling positive energy and dissipating negative energy.

Destiny and its Formation

"You can't connect the dots looking forward; you can only connect them looking backwards. So, you have to trust that the dots will somehow connect in your future. You have to trust in something—your gut, destiny, life, karma, whatever. This approach has never let me down, and it has made all the difference in my life."

—STEVE JOBS

Destiny sometimes referred to as fate (from the Latin *fatum)*, is a predetermined course of events. It may be conceived as a predetermined future, whether in general or of an individual.

Destiny is formed by different factors, some under control and some not. Whatever you are today is not only because of the way you think and act now. It is a combination of five different imprints.

Let's examine each one:

1. **Your surroundings**: Knowingly and unknowingly, you learn many things from your surroundings. The process of learning starts from the early age of two when you start grasping things around you. In the initial years, your grasping power is very high. As per a study, whatever you are today is conditioned from the learning gained till the age of five!

2. **This Birth's karma***: Whatever good and bad you think and do creates your destiny. Thus, good karma produces a good effect, while bad karma produces a bad effect. This effect may be material, moral or emotional — that is, one's karma affects one's happiness and unhappiness. If you have the habit of waking up early in the morning and doing physical activity, you are creating your destiny of remaining healthy in your old age. If you smoke many cigarettes a day, you are creating a destiny of poor health.

3. **Genetic impact:** When a child is born, the genes are transmitted from parents to offspring. These genes carry traits not only from the parents but also from relatives like grandparents, uncles, aunts, etc. In terms of genes, a child does not have control over them but must carry them with him/her from birth. You must have seen many persons whose hair gets grey in the teenage age although they do not have any health ailment, that is generally due to genetic impact.

---

* **Karma:** the sum of a person's actions in this and previous states of existence, viewed as deciding one's fate in future existences.

4. **Past birth:** Karma is the Divine Law of Justice that applies to all of us. It's a LAW, just like the Law of Gravity. Doing Good gives us good results and doing bad gives bad results. This Law has existed forever, acting automatically in all our past incarnations; and it is acting on you in this birth. Sometimes, you wonder why bad things are happening to you even when you haven't committed any sin…It's your past life's bad karma catching up with you (like a flood or earthquake). THAT person was also you; THIS person is also you. Similarly, you will find persons who may not be very intelligent & deserving but still, all the best things in the world may be happening with them. The classic example is the birth of twins. Although they are identical in terms of birth time and physical appearance, still they are two entirely different personalities.

5. **Original impressions:** These are the original impressions of the soul that are pure and without taint when our journey started.

Thus, you are the sum total of five different imprints. The question is what is in your control and what is not? Original impressions, past birth and genetic impact are not in your control. Only two factors are controllable, i.e. your surroundings and your karmas in this birth. You have limited control over your surroundings (at least during childhood), but you have 100% control over your karmas. Whatever you feed in makes your karmas, it is imperative to take care of what you absorb. Maybe in childhood you weren't aware and did not have much control; but as you grew into an adult, it became your responsibility to take care of what you are feeding in consciously and unconsciously. The kind of self-talk that you do, the type of people you meet, the kind of food you eat, etc. make your present karmas.

If you are born with bad genes and poor karmas, what can you do now to improve? You cannot delete anything from your past, but you can certainly dilute things by doing more and more good karmas.

You are the creator of your destiny. You may have many pitfalls, but you are the owner of your destiny. The onus lies with you.

The Purpose of Self-Talk

"If we start to ask ourselves the right questions, it would change everything. Empowering questions unleash your ability to take action and express who you really are"
—JOSEPH MURPHY

In 24 hours, we create more than 45,000 thoughts. You are generating all these thoughts consciously or unconsciously (mostly). Your thoughts make you the person you are today. When you have the capability to create negative thoughts in your mind, you also have equal power and opportunity to create positive thoughts.

Self-Talk helps change our habits slowly but steadily; the intent is to reprogram our subconscious mind to new programs. Example: you are making tea and you add more sugar than needed. You cannot remove sugar from the tea but you can always dilute the sugar by adding more water or milk. Self-Talk intends to dilute existing Sanskars* to a new set. You cannot actually remove them, but you can dilute them by adding a different flavour.

The purpose of self-talk is to

♦ **Make yourselves strong:** Many times, you find yourselves vulnerable to others. Vulnerability is a good thing provided you have control over it and other people don't misuse it. When you do not feel confident, you present your meek character to the world. To overcome such a situation, you need to identify the cause of this weakness and work through it. Self-Talk is a wonderful medicine that works magically to cure your wounds.

♦ **Do what you want:** It is good to be flexible and adjustable to a situation. But at times, one's flexibility is considered a weakness. People around you start utilizing your flexibility to their benefit, which is fine. But when you start realizing that your flexibility is inhibiting your growth, as it is considered a weakness and not strength, you need to find a solution. Self-Talk helps to bring us out of such a situation and realize our true potential.

♦ **Correct your thinking:** You are always surrounded by people. Most speak negatively about every situation. A few days back, I wished a friend "Happy Birthday". When I asked him, "How was last year?" his response was, "Nothing special. Still alive." Then I asked him a

---

* *Sanskars are dispositions, character or behavioural traits, that exist as default from birth or are prepared and perfected by a person over one's lifetime as imprints on the subconscious*
            —According to various schools of hindu philosophy.

few questions, "How is your health, how is your job, how is the family?" To all the questions, he replied, "Everything is fine." But still, he was not energetic when saying everything was fine. There is so much negativity around us that we need a protective layer to prevent us from being affected. Self-Talk is that tool.

♦ **Ask the right question:** One potent method of keeping our minds healthy is to ask the "right questions'. Some of the general questions: are you ok, will you be on time, is it very hot outside or can you complete this task? The answer to all these questions will be negative. It is important to ask the right questions to get a positive response like I am always on time, I am healthy, I enjoy all kinds of weather, I always complete my tasks. Self-Talk helps us correct our vocabulary.

To imbibe the above points in your nature, you need to work on your subconscious mind. Your subconscious mind does not understand anything as Good or Bad. It is pure and innocent. It does not differentiate or know what you are feeding it. Whatever you feed in will be stored and become a permanent citizen. When you do self-Talk, you are in a conscious state. You know what you are doing intentionally. You are sending signals to your subconscious mind to change a particular habit. But your subconscious mind is an adamant creature! It does not easily allow anything to come in or leave!

If you say, I always forget my keys, it is *not* easy for your subconscious mind to accept the original script that you are a superpower. The *security guard* sitting in front of your subconscious mind is extremely powerful. It does not let in or let out anything easily. Although it is lazy, it is also very obedient. But, when you continuously feed your mind with thoughts and words like, I forget my keys, you force your subconscious mind to change. It has no option but to accept what you are feeding in.

Through consistent self-talk (positive & negative), you make sure that the *security guard* allows new thoughts to germinate without discrimination. But there is one problem with the subconscious mind. It works in binary mode (0 or 1, good or bad, hot or cold). When one thought germinates, the security guard releases another, "My memory is very sharp and I always remember to keep my keys or no one loves me" without any emotional attachment.

SUMMARY

- **What is Self-Talk?** Self-Talk is an internal monologue or inner speech. According to a study, on average, we have 45000 to 55000 thoughts in a day which translates into 25 to 35 thoughts a minute. It means that our minds keep on fluctuating throughout the day. Like breathing, this is a normal process over which you do not seem to have any control. Self-Talk plays a dominant role in deciding how to direct your thoughts.

- **My experience with Self-Talk:** In your day-to-day life, you are doing self-talk without bothering about its content. At the end of the day, generally, you may be finding yourself exhausted. You might be wondering why you are feeling exhausted although you have not done any heavy stuff. Over the years, I realized that self-talk is a powerful tool that creates an aura around us. If the aura is positive, you think you can do anything in the world.

- **Our conscious mind** is the active mind that observes and does everything with attention. It has the power to make the decision. It is the "watchman at the gate." Its chief function is to protect our subconscious mind from false impressions.

- **Our subconscious mind** is subjective. It has unlimited potential. The subconscious mind's function is to store everything and retrieve it when needed. It never grows old and is extremely powerful. We just need to feed something into it, practice it every-day and it becomes part of us.

■ **Vibrations** are nothing but a form of energy which transforms from one form to another. At times we do not realize its importance but actually, it is extremely potent just like a simple birthday greeting prepared by your 5-year kid, which has no extrinsic value but most valuable to you as a parent.

■ **Destiny and its formation** are based on 5 things which include your surroundings, this birth karma, genetic impact, past birth & original impressions. We do have little control over the majority of them except our surroundings and this birth karmas.

■ **The Purpose of Self-Talk** is to make yourself strong, to do what you want, to correct your thinking and to ask the right questions. This is possible by working on your subconscious mind which works in binary mode.

THINGS TO PONDER

(a) Observe your inner chatter and see what kind of thoughts you create knowingly & unknowingly.

(b) Do you have any control over your inner chatter?

(c) Could you differentiate when your conscious mind or subconscious mind is working?

(d) If Self-Talk is helping you or distracting you?

CHAPTER
3
Types of Self-Talk

How to do Self-Talk?

There is no definite formula to making self-talk. You need to identify what you want from your life and put it down in detail on a piece of paper or in a digital medium or just remember it. Once it is written, reduce it to two or three lines.

Once a summary is made, you can start using it. Very soon you will realize whether you are comfortable chanting it or not. If not, you can modify it and make it simpler. There is nothing like "the BEST Self-Talk." Whatever self-talk works for you, is the best self-talk.

If you think that you are procrastinating a lot which results in delaying work beyond the time limit, you can devise a small self-talk like

I always plan my work

I complete my work as per my plan

I strongly believe that completing work on time is awesome

I fully trust in my planning

With the above self-talk, you can create wonders for yourself. The science behind it is that you are reprograming your subconscious mind continually. Thus, whenever an occasion arises where you are trying to delay something, say, paying a credit card bill on time, your subconscious mind will say, "Why do you want to pay your credit card bill so early; you still have seven days." Since you are in the process of reconditioning your subconscious mind, your conscious mind (regularly activated by your self-talk) will become active and say

> I *always plan my work*
>
> I *complete my work per my plan*
>
> I *strongly believe that completing work on time is awesome*
>
> I *fully trust in my planning*

You will have the opportunity to make the call whether to pay your bill today or later. Earlier, your subconscious mind was very strong, instructing you to delay. But now your conscious mind is activated and will offer an alternative option. At least you have the option to choose between the two which did not exist before! There is a high probability that you choose *not* to pay and delay again, but it is fine as you have at least initiated a process of change. As you continue to do your self-talk every day several times, you activate your mind for change. A few days later, you will get a reminder that the due date for paying bills is tomorrow. Again, your ever-loyal subconscious will tell you, "So what, you still have ONE more day; you can do it tomorrow."

This time, however, your activated conscious mind will send you a signal to submit your bills today even though you still have one more day. There is a good possibility that your trusted old friend (the subconscious mind) may again compel you to delay payment. But somewhere your subconscious mind is getting a signal that not everything is right and someone is pushing it to change!

There is a very high chance that this month at least you will make the payments by the last day and not default! Throughout the month, the tussle between your charged-up conscious and lazy subconscious mind will continue. If you persist with your journey of self-talk, next month when the deadline for paying credit cards looms, the chance of submitting it much before the last day will be very high. This is the way self-talk becomes a process of winning *yourself* over from the inner self recurrently.

As discussed in the previous example about procrastination, another common thought process is that "I forget my keys," we can devise small and powerful self-talk to dilute previous *Sanskars*.

My memory is very sharp

I remember everything

I have full control over my memory

My memory is very sharp

Just like we have the power to create negative thoughts, we are equally powerful to create positive thoughts. When we start chanting the above self-talk through our conscious minds, we are again reminding our subconscious to consider new thoughts. Although the security guard is extremely merciless, we still have a chance to overturn an existing thought pattern.

As discussed in many books, there are different theories regarding the number of times and days needed to change a habit by working on the subconscious mind. You can follow any theory you like. The end objective is to manage your habits through the power of self-talk.

There are various ways of doing self-talk:

♦ verbal

♦ written

♦ recorded

♦ non-verbal

Each type of self-talk has its own merits. People have their comfort level for each kind. All have a definite purpose. When we start doing self-talk, it is pertinent to know what difference we want to make in our lives. Accordingly, we must choose. At times, we may want to do a combination of self-talk like verbal and written or verbal and listening, or different combinations of two or more. It does not make any difference what type of self-talk we chose.

The important point is to decide and visualize what we want to achieve and the type of self-talk working for us. There is no definite formula for what kinds of words we need to speak or write. What matters is the method that works for you. There are many people for whom self-talk works only when they write it down. They feel the confidence once they have written their self-talk several times, it registers better in their mind. The younger generation that is mainly on digital platforms may not like the idea of writing. For them, maybe listening to audio self-talk is more compatible.

If I had to share my preference, it would be verbal self-talk. It suits me and is working great.

Verbal Self-Talk

In verbal self-talk, you repeat certain golden words that you want to absorb in your life. As stated earlier, our *habits* are formed by *actions*. Our *actions* are the result of what we *think*. What we *think* is created by the kind of *input* we give to our *minds* throughout the day. So, we need to plan a verbal self-talk that will impact our minds.

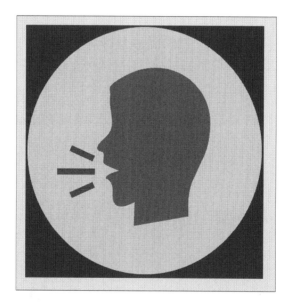

Our habits are formed by the consistent and persistent effort we make for any trait (good or bad). In case you want to replace or create any habit, you need to work at the mind level. Whatever you throw into it regularly and religiously will be converted into thoughts. Thoughts will push you to act. Whatever action you will take regularly will make new or modified habits.

I have experimented with myself many times. I always wanted to be a stage performer but whenever I used to be on stage, I forever struggled with words. My mouth would get dry, the mind used to go blank and I could never deliver what I wanted to. So, I stopped raising my hand for any query requiring me to face the audience or stage. But I was losing my position in the organization and less experienced or incompetent personnel were getting ahead of me. I had to do something to fix this problem. Whenever I was with a group of people, where there was a possibility of raising my hand and speaking in front of them, I used to chant the following lines continuously.

I am the best

I can do it

I believe in myself

I know I can do it

These few words used to work magic for me. They created an aura around me that I am capable of raising my hand and speaking in front of people. It has worked wonders for many years.

You need to create your own words that work for you. Maybe my words work wonders for me only! Whatever words you think work for you, keep on chanting them. Very soon, you will realize that you have the power to face the situation. The trick for improving performance on stage is "to be on stage as many times as possible." The more you are on stage, the better your self-confidence will be. Verbal self-talk can be utilized for solving any of life's challenge.

Written Self-Talk

An ancient proverb about writing:

"The palest ink is stronger than the sharpest memory."

Just like verbal self-talk, written self-talk is equally powerful and brings desired results. For many of us, unless we write something on a piece of paper, we do not own it. When you write, you are not only verbalizing it, but you are engraving it on the screen of your mind. You must know that there are four different stages of learning anything. They are listening, speaking, reading and writing. You must have observed that writing has been specified as the last stage but when we listen, speak, read and write, our learning is complete.

Whenever you want to prepare self-talk, write down a summary of what you want to do. Once done, you can summarize it in a few lines. Maybe you want to prepare self-talk for healthy food habits. You can write

I always eat healthy food

When I eat healthy food, I get energized

I am fond of health food

I feel excited about eating healthy food

It is important to note that the content of self-talk should be precise and to the point. If its too long, it may bore you. Let it be crisp and clear. You need to define a time frame when you will be using this self-talk. Just like the habit of having tea/coffee at a defined interval, you need to decide when you will be writing your self-talk. When you write self-talk at a planned time, it signals your mind that you are doing an important job and are serious about it. If you do not write consistently, you give a confusing signal to your mind that your self-talk is not important for consideration.

When you write, you are not only articulating it in your mind, but you are also creating a picture of how healthy you want to feel and look. Your subconscious mind is like a bank, a sort of universal financial institution. It magnifies whatever you deposit or impress upon it whether it be the idea of being healthy or unhealthy. When you visualize that you are healthy, your subconscious mind starts searching and suggesting ways by which good health can be maintained. It could be healthy food, Yoga, going to the gym, avoiding junk food and many more options. When your mind starts giving you options, you tend to pick anyone which suits you. Maybe, in the beginning, the response may be slow but more you practice writing self-talk, you create more possibility of applying healthy ways of living. Let me share my personal experience.

I am fond of drinking tea many times a day. I always had a perception about myself that it is just hot water mixed with some ingredients and nothing more. I am *not* addicted to it and I can leave it whenever I want. I continued with my belief for many years. Gradually what was supposed to be a habit under my control became an addiction. Then I decided to challenge myself and see whether I could spend an entire day without tea. I created a small self-talk for the same.

I enjoy drinking tea

I decide when to drink it

I can stop whenever I want

I can start whenever I want

I practised the self-talk for a few weeks and decided that every week on Tuesday, I will not drink tea. In the beginning, I used to forget that Tuesdays are no-tea days. But, as I continued with my self-talk, not only did I remember not to drink on Tuesday but I also conquered my inner dependency on it. My only objective of this written self-talk was to create an eco-system around me where *I am deciding my habits*!!

When you write your self-talk, it is important to feel that you have achieved what you are writing. It is vital to understand that merely writing self-talk will not work wonders, but when you start feeling that you have already achieved your goal, it triggers your conscious mind to create new images in your subconscious. The conviction with which you write is beneficial for your affirmations*.

Recorded Self-Talk

In this fast-paced life where everyone is running from pillar to post, it is very difficult to find time to write or verbalize self-talk. Especially now when digitalization is happening at lightning speed, many are looking for a digital medium

---

* Affirmation means something which is already firm and we are re-firming (reconfirming) it in our subconscious mind.

to improve their skillset. Recording self-talk on tape and listening to it is an old practice.

With the advent of tools like mobile phones, tablets, Pen Drive, Bluetooth, and MP3, it has become very easy to record and transfer information. It is convenient to record self-talk of your choice and just put earphones on and enjoy listening. When you are writing or verbalizing self-talk, generally it is compact in content but in a digital medium, you can increase the scale as you like.

There are many readymade self-talks available on a digital medium like YouTube where you can listen online or download offline and listen whenever it is convenient. Though the preferable option is to create *your own* self-talk. Even though we all have similar problems, each one of us is a unique creature. It is recommended to create self-talk of your own.

When you listen to your recorded self-talk religiously, it gets registered in your subconscious mind. Even if you continue to listen, to the recorded self-talk while engaged in work, the self-talk will serve its purpose. Your objective is not to change your conscious mind but your subconscious. Active attention is not *always* needed.

Say you have a Sanskars of speaking lies and have recorded the following self-talk.

I always speak the truth

I feel confident when I speak the truth

Speaking truth is in my nature

Speaking truth comes naturally to me

With the above self-talk, you are priming your subconscious mind that you always speak the truth. Whenever you face a scenario where you feeling more comfortable telling a lie, your subconscious mind will prompt you to think before doing it and will offer you another option.

Example: You are in the office and your superior gives you a task which is to be completed within a specified timeframe. You are then asked, "Have you completed your task?" If you have the habit of speaking lies, you will confidently say, 'Yes, I did'. If you are not happy with your present state and want to change it, you can start listening to the above self-talk regularly.

In a few weeks, if your superior asks the same question, this time instead of blatantly saying, yes when the answer should be No, two choices will appear in front of you: the truth or not. This possibility has been created by consistently listening to self- talk prompting your inner voice to consider two answers instead of simply saying Yes. Even if you respond *incorrectly*, you will feel satisfied that you had two options. When you *own* the responsibility of speaking lies, your inner conscious will question your decision.

The good part of the above process is that at least you came out of autopilot mode and have started creating choices, which *you* own. Once this process is triggered, you are on the path of improvement. The possibility of changing your Sanskars increases. As you continue listening to the self-talk regularly, a stage will come when you will not feel like speaking lies. Internally, you will start posing questions to yourself like, "Why can't I complete my work on time, why do I need to speak lies, and what will happen if I speak the truth." With the strength of positive self-talk, you will not only empower yourself to speak the truth, but you are also questioning your habit of delaying work, which is prompting you to speak lies.

Once you reach this stage, you can review your earlier self-talk and create an improved version like

> *I always complete my tasks on time*
>
> *I always plan things in advance*
>
> *Whenever someone asks me something, I am ready with a solution*
>
> *Everyone appreciates that I complete my tasks on time*
>
> *As the situation has changed, modified self-talk will do wonders for your performance.*

Non-verbal Self-Talk

The non-verbal type is the most powerful self-talk we do day and night. It can be positive or negative. We do not even realize how frequently we are doing it unconsciously and unintentionally.

You can attribute your *today* to your non-verbal self-talk. In your day-to-day life, your mood swings from 'wow' to 'why.' Some nonverbal talks are voluntary and many just happen! At times, your mood swings to low and sometimes it continues for weeks, months and years. Few times, you feel bubbly throughout the day. You may be getting excited, demoralized, depressed, charged up, emotional, shaken, anxious, fearful, possessive or other mental states. All the examples below are the experiences we have in our life. You do not need to exchange a word but the impact is so powerful that it becomes a part of your destiny. Thus, it is very important to monitor your non-verbal chitchat. Let me share a few examples of non-verbal self-talk that has impacted *my* life.

Charged up: I still remember an incident when I was going to my office by local bus. During those days, I used to be quite negative about myself. My energy level was always low. I was not happy about how my career was shaping up and I blamed others for my condition all the time. All of a sudden, I saw one rickshaw puller (a tricycle used to ferry passengers manually) carrying three passengers, pulling the rickshaw paddle with one leg (the other was amputated). He was graciously smiling and driving.

I was shocked! This guy with one leg was pulling three passengers in a manual rickshaw and here I am cribbing about little things. All of a sudden, my slackness went away. I thanked God for being kind to me and keeping me healthy. My body language changed and my state of mind improved drastically.

Excited: At one point in time, I was afraid of speaking in front of a group of people. I used to be terrified although I often spoke when it was unavoidable. For my organization, I had to start a series of small training for the workers. But the idea of speaking in front of a group was holding up my decision, although it was important for my self-growth.

One day, I was going to my office and boarded the bus near my house. After a few minutes, I saw a young guy (a medical representative of a Pharmaceuticals company) addressing a small group of his colleagues (5 to 6 in number) on the pedestrian way. This guy used to be a shy kid and was known to me. I told myself if he can do it then I can: I am much better than him. Why I am delaying my decision? Non-verbal self-talk triggered my mind and I decided to initiate the training program from that day onward. It was the seed I needed to grow my upcoming public training.

Possessive: On 8th November of 2016, demonetization was announced by the Indian government. With immediate effect, currency notes of 500 and 1000 were demonetized. Throughout the country, there was hue and cry. Everything came to a standstill. To exchange to the new currency, there were long, unending queues outside every bank. Currency notes of a denomination lower than 100, 50 and 10 became very precious. Since in India most of the money transactions are through hard currency, every single currency note became important.

I vividly remember that for many months after this, when I would pull out my wallet to make payments, I was always scared that someone would snatch the wallet from me. Although that fear did not linger for more than a year, the possessiveness toward currency notes continued even today. This was the impact of the non-verbal self-talk that triggered my mind without my knowledge.

Demoralized: When you think you are committed to a particular project, you become sincere about doing your job. You focus all your attention and energy in resolving a query. During this intense process, if someone finds fault with your intentions, it dents your morale. You get demoralized. I vividly remember an incident that happened to me around ten years back, when I was trying to do my job well, putting 100% into it. My senior scolded me for losing a project to a competitor.

I had put my best efforts into retaining the business, but somehow this client did not continue doing business with us and shifted to a competitor. I did not like the attitude of my senior who was not looking at the overall picture and the achievements I had brought to the company. I was questioned for losing one project. I was demoralized and it took many weeks to realize that my mind had taken a wrong path (negative self-talk) and I had overreacted to his response.

Fearful: *Fear is the anticipation of pain. The fastest ways to release any fear is to accept the pain that you might feel as a result of taking action.* We have all observed and realized that "negative attracts negative and positive attracts positive." I have observed in very hilarious and funny situations how many times our internal self-talk creates different situations for the same cause. You must have noticed stray dogs barking in the road. You must have also noticed that passersby who are fearful of dogs will stop at a distance and try to figure out if there is any danger in crossing the road.

Sometimes these fearful passersby shout at the dogs while crossing. There is a very high possibility that the dogs will bark at them and even follow them. From another perspective, you must have seen passersby who will cross by the dogs, ignoring their fear that the dogs will bark or chase them. Have you ever thought about why this happens? When you are fearful, you pass the vibration that you are afraid, and the dogs will respond by barking or rushing at you. For the other passersby who do not give a damn, the dogs do not care. So, our non-verbal self-talk creates both challenges and comfort for us.

Emotional: We feel emotional in different situations. Sometimes when we are watching a movie, we get emotional. During my college days, when we used to watch movies, one friend used to start weeping whenever he watched a marriage sequence with the bride leaving her home and parents. He started relating it to his sister who was to be married soon. In this situation, no one was talking to anyone but the non-verbal communication was so strong that he got emotional.

Anxious: It is a very common symptom for most people. In any situation, the possibility of getting anxious is very high. I have seen it happen when watching sports. Just like football is the biggest sport in many countries, cricket is extremely popular in India. Whenever the country is quite close to winning or losing, the spectators get anxious about the results. Some do not even change their sitting position as they fear it may not be a good omen for the team. We start chewing our nails and do not even realize it by the time the match ends. Nonverbal self-talk works mysteriously!

Depression: There is an adage: *"behind every grey cloud is a silver lining."* But depression is a mental disorder that is catching many of us. We do not even realize that we are depressed. When things do not go our way and we do not have a social structure or mechanism to overcome the fear of losing or not getting what we want, we slip into depression. This is the most dangerous output of non-verbal self-talk.

SUMMARY

■ **How to do Self-Talk?** There is no definite formula to making self-talk. The sole objective of having small self-talk is that it will be easy to remember and repeat. There are different type of Self-Talk (Verbal, Written, Recorded, Non-Verbal). Each type of self-talk has its own merits. The important point is what we want to achieve and what type of self-talk is working for us.

■ **Verbal Self-Talk:** In verbal self-talk, you repeat certain golden words that you want to absorb in your life. You need to create your own words that work for you. Verbal self-talk can be utilized for solving any of life's challenge.

■ **Written Self-Talk:** It is very powerful and brings the desired results. For many of us, unless we write something on a piece of paper, we do not own it. When you write, you are not only verbalizing it, but you are engraving it on the screen of your mind. When you write your self-talk, it is important to feel that you have achieved what you are writing. The conviction with which you write is beneficial for your affirmations.

■ **Recorded Self-Talk:** With the advent of tools like mobile phones, tablets, Pen Drive, Bluetooth, and MP3, it has become very easy to record and transfer information. It is convenient to record self-talk of your choice and just put earphones on and enjoy listening. Even if when are busy doing some work, if you continue to listen, the self-talk will serve its purpose. Your objective is not to change your conscious mind but your subconscious. Active attention is not always needed.

■ **Non-Verbal Self-Talk:** The non-verbal type is the most powerful self-talk we do day and night. It can be positive or negative. We do not even realize how frequently we are doing it unconsciously and unintentionally. You may be getting excited, demoralized, depressed, charged up, emotional, shaken, anxious, fearful, possessive or other mental states.

THINGS TO PONDER

(a) How you do your Self-Talk—Verbal, Non-Verbal, Recorded or Written Self-Talk?

(b) Which Self-Talk is more effective for you?

(c) Is it positive or negative?

CHAPTER

4

Negative Self-Talk

Types of Negative Self-Talk

Negative self-talk is any thought that diminishes you, your confidence and your ability to make positive changes in life.

From childhood, knowingly and unknowingly, we start creating different types of negative expressions which later turn into negative self-talk (inner chattering). These negative expressions primarily result from

♦ our environment

♦ our habits

♦ heredity

We do have some control over our environment and our habits but not over our heredity! We don't realize that we catch the infection of negative expressions from our surroundings. Slowly and steadily, these expressions become a part of our personality. This negative self-talk can be broadly categorized into seven parts:

♦ overreaction

♦ comparison

♦ personalization

♦ absolute language

♦ assumption

♦ expectations

♦ regret

Overreaction: Sometimes, we react more emotionally or forcefully than what is justified. For example, your wife is learning to drive a car and you are helping her with it. If she bumps the car against a roadside tree, you may start shouting, which may not be justified although you made similar and even more mistakes while learning to drive. Sometimes in the office, when a colleague makes a mistake, we behave as if something catastrophic has happened, although we may be doing much worse ourselves.

Comparison: We compare ourselves with others and create feelings of superiority or inferiority within. From "likes" on Facebook, to financial earnings, to the degree of power and influence and even skin tone, we compare ourselves with others in almost every aspect of life imaginable.

Personalization: Sometimes, we start taking responsibility for something that does not belong to us or we don't have enough control over. For example, if my child is not performing well in studies, I may consider myself responsible for it's failure. As a cricket coach, if my team does not perform well, I consider myself responsible for their failure and feel guilty about it.

Absolute language: If the team (that you're a part of) does not perform well, you squarely take the blame for it. Your inner chatter goes like **I am responsible for the failure and no one else.** Instead of "the colour of my skin is black" your inner chatter spurts out, I AM BLACK. Instead of "I have fat on my body", you mentally say out loud, I AM FAT.

Assumption: It is a thing accepted as truth or certain to happen without any proof. When a boy sends a message to his girlfriend, and doesn't receive a response as her phone's battery has died, the boy assumes that she doesn't like him. Or, you write an email to your boss about your annual vacation but he does not respond. You get irritated or scared but maybe your boss missed your mail.

Expectations: These are belief about what might happen in the future. During football World Cup matches, citizens of every country expect theirs to win. Sometimes, we have very high expectations of our children to take care of us in our old age but at times it doesn't come true.

Regret: When we feel sad or repentant about something, it is very common to talk about the house we could have bought but did not due to the high cost; but now we regret our decision. In our college days, we might have thought of proposing to a girl but could not out of fear of rejection; but now after so many years, we are regretting what we could have done at that time.

All of the above are an expression of negative chatter that goes on within us knowingly and unknowingly. They create a negative aura around us.

Why do we Create Negative Self-Talk?

One of the key reasons for creating negative self-talk is our insecurities towards life. From early childhood, seeds of negativity are fed by our surroundings (Parents, neighbours, Friends, Teachers, Media etc.). When 3 to 4 years old kids do not listen to their parents, than the kids are fed with scary statements like "ghost will come and pick you or police will come and take you away or you will be locked in the room alone." When a child is carrying your expensive mobile phone, you do not say "carry it carefully.", instead you tell the child "the phone may fall." This approach is used by parents and elders not once but many times in different situations. We don't teach our children 'to speak truth' but we tell them "do not speak lies." We do not guide our children to be attentive, we tell them "not to be distracted." As per a study, by the time a child reaches the age of 14 years, negative words have been fed to the child thousands of times. With such a diet, children are bound to create negative self-talk. It is rightly said that whatever is done repeatedly becomes a part of us (Garbage in – Garbage out).

Garbage in

> *"The mind is restless, turbulent, strong and unyielding; it is as difficult to control it as it is to control the wind."*
> —BHAGAVAD GITA VERSE 6.34

This is the single most important aspect that designs life. We always think about why things are happening this way or that. Sometimes we think that life is favouring us, but at times we think otherwise. The pertinent question is WHY does it happen?

From years of experience, I have observed that the root cause is what we *take in* every day. It is just like the farmer who is sowing potatoes in his field. The output will be potatoes, even if the present market requirement is for onions. So, it is very important to understand that *"what you sow, so shall you reap."*

In case we think that the market requirement is for onions, we need to anticipate it in advance. Otherwise, we will repent in the end that things are not happening the way we want. Thus, throughout the day, it is important to comprehend what we are taking in. Let us see a typical scenario of our everyday life.

— Starting in the morning on Monday, as soon as we wake up our first reaction is, *"Oh shit, it's Monday again, it sucks."* Then we realize that we had set the alarm for 6:00 am but we have woken at 6.30 am. Another thought comes to mind, *"I cannot wake up on time. This has been the problem with me since past many years, I will not improve."*

— Then you find that your wife is waking the child and is still struggling. Another thought comes to you, *"My kid is just like me, lethargic."*

— When you go to freshen up in the bathroom, you do not get the desired results!! Another thought comes, *"It's in my genes. We all have the same problem in the morning."*

— You need to drop your kid at the school bus. Since you are late, you are walking fast, carrying your child's 5 kg school bag while yelling at yourself, *"Is it the kind of morning I expected."*

— As you are late reaching the school bus — it was about to leave — you need to yell at the bus driver to stop.

— By the time you are back home, you realize that you are late leaving for the office. Somehow you manage to get ready, but you don't have time for breakfast. You think, let's skip it today. As you are driving your car to the office on a Monday morning, you find a lot of traffic. By the time you reach it, you have yelled so much at the poor traffic management and how people drive that your energy level is down 50%.

— As the day progresses, you have some heated argument with your boss (obviously one-sided), *you are cribbing about the whole system of doing your job and the kind of cruelty that bosses exert on their employees.* During lunch, your favourite topic is to criticize the organization, bosses, present government and everyone else.

— By the time your day ends, *your* battery is almost dead. You talk to yourself and say, *"why did I work like a donkey throughout the day?"* After reaching home, apart from yelling again at the traffic and drivers, you also criticize God for the mess in your life.

— You sit in front of the TV to have dinner, enjoying the latest political news only to find faults with politicians, moaning about what they should and should not do. Since you are extremely tired, physically and mentally, you tend to *relax* by drinking alcohol and signing off for the day.

This is the way your day ends. It is important to understand how much garbage was *taken in* throughout the day and what will happen the next: the same story will be repeated and you will think, why does this happen to me only!!

Garbage out

I read a newspaper article some years ago that told about a horse who had shied when he came to a stump in the road. Subsequently, every time the horse came to that same stump, he shied. The farmer dug the stump out, burned it, and levelled the old road. Yet, for twenty-five years, every time the horse passed the place where the former stump was, he shied. The horse was shying at the memory of the stump. Sometimes, due to fear long back, we remain afraid for our entire lives!!

—ANONYMOUS

So, throughout the day, we take "garbage in". What will happen to this garbage? It will certainly be processed in our memories and the output will be the same as what we had *put in*. We keep on adding this garbage every day without realizing the crime we are committing to ourselves.

— The next day when alarm rings, the first thought that crosses our minds is, *"oh its morning again, I have still not completed my sleep; let me have more time."* By the time you get out of bed, you are late again. As your child is still not getting ready for school on time, your wife is screaming.

— Now, your mind reconfirms the thought, *"my kid is lethargic like me."* Since you are missing your child's school bus, you have a premonition that today you will catch the bus by running after it. Once again you are cementing thoughts of negativity. Rushing to the office in traffic and finding a similar situation makes you believe that nothing can be done about the traffic and how people drive.

— In the office, too, the boss will ask for some urgent information and your mind will tell you that bosses are always bad and they never try to understand the perspectives of their employees. During lunch, you find everyone cribbing about the performance of the present government and you tend to believe that everything is wrong around you.

— As the day ends and you feel fully exhaustive, you recall the same feeling on previous days, the one that says, "*am I a donkey?*" Reaching home, you again sit in front of the TV, watching crass news on a different channel. Since you are again tired, you want to relax with alcohol as it worked for you in the previous night. And so, the saga continues, "garbage in, garbage out".

It is very important to understand that this vicious circle is never-ending. Without realizing it, most of us are completely entangled in it. Since we find this pattern in the majority, we tend to realize that it is reality.

In the same vein, if anyone is detected with high blood pressure or too much blood sugar in their thirties or forties, the general perception is, "*it is ok, it is very common these days.*" Something uncommon has become the norm. Rather than questioning the wrong pattern or saving ourselves from it, we become a part of it. The more we start believing in it, the more we get entrapped.

Thus, it is important to understand how we can save ourselves from negativity. The more we avoid generating wrong thoughts for ourselves and others, the better off we will be. The important question is, "what do we do to get rid of the garbage, so we can enjoy the life we want and see it from a positive perspective?"

Repetition

"The question is not what you look at, but what you see"
— HENRY DAVID THOREAU

One common factor in our habits, whether good or bad, is how repeatedly we do them. Anything done repeatedly becomes a habit. When we were talking about garbage in garbage out, the reason why garbage is coming out is that we keep on repeating the same pattern again and again.

When we say, *"Monday morning sucks,"* we are sending a signal to our mind that Monday morning is not good. We do it when we wake up when sitting with friends and many more times throughout the day. We repeat the same thing: I do not like Monday morning as I have to go to work. You get the same signal from your friends who agree with your point of view. They share many instances reaffirming to you that *Monday morning sucks.*

> *I need to go to the office again*
>
> *I have to see my boss' face again*
>
> *The rut of life begins again*

We are repeatedly giving the same signal to our minds such that after a few weeks, irrespective of whether that particular Monday is pleasant or not, we will still feel that *Monday morning sucks.*

It is not only *we* who are getting affected by this repeated self-talk but also the persons surrounding us. . If you are married, your spouse undoubtedly shares their feelings about Monday mornings being bad. Your child too, gets affected by this negative talk. He also asks, *"why do I need to go to school on Monday; I have not completed my homework; I will not be able to play games with friends (like on his mobile phone, Playstation, etc.!)."*

Sometimes we may say something relevant to ourselves but how we are pronouncing it makes a difference to our state of mind. Like

Why am I so unhappy? You will be unhappy most of the time.

Why am I so broke? You find a way not to have money, even when money comes in.

Why can't I lose weight? You find it hard to lose weight, no matter what you try.

Why can't I do anything right? You focus on what goes wrong and ignore the things you do right.

Why am I tired and retired? You will feel a lack of energy and motivation.

Why am I not good at relationships? You will start questioning your most intimate relationship.

Why am I unpredictable? You will begin to question your credibility.

Why am I not beautiful? You will start comparing yourself with others and degrading yourself.

Why do people not love me? You will start questioning the intentions of your dear ones.

Looking at the above statements, you can observe that even though you are asking yourself a relevant and pertinent question, the intent is *negative*. When the intention is not right, the possible responses from your subconscious mind will be negative. When you say, *"Why can't I lose weight?"*, you are generating negative answers like

> *I eat too much*
>
> *I don't do physical activity*
>
> *I am lazy*
>
> *I have tried earlier but always failed*
>
> *I have seen people lose weight but they regain it again*

When responses are negative, you get bogged down by them.

When you store negative thoughts in your mind, you start believing that way. Someone has rightly said, *"Our thoughts make our life; our life does not make our thoughts."* Like

> *speaking lies*
>
> *smoking cigarette*
>
> *using abusive words*
>
> *believing one is less competent*
>
> *disbelieving in ones success*

When you start telling lies, you might feel uncomfortable at the beginning, but as you keep repeating them, you will become comfortable in telling lies and feel like a master of lies!

When you start smoking cigarettes, you might hide it from others in the beginning but after a few weeks, you start feeling that when so many people are smoking in the open, why should I hide my habit. That little insecurity which was holding you back that you *are not* doing the right thing becomes a thing of the past.

When you proudly say, I am broke, you may think you are making fun of yourself. But you do not realize that in the process, you have started believing that you are broke. You will start behaving like a broke person; and soon, you will be attracted to activities that will make you broke!

When you start using abusive words, you create an aura around you, where speaking them becomes a part of your normal life and you do not have any guilt about it.

When you start saying, I am less competent than others, you will always find something good in others and something bad in yourself. The more you find a gap in yourself, the more you will feel disempowered and incompetent.

When you say, I am not good with relationships, you are giving a signal to yourself and others that you cannot be trusted. The habit of breaking off a relationship becomes strong no matter who comes into close contact with you. You will become fearful about how long you will be able to continue the relationship.

The more you think that you are not beautiful, the more you are making yourself a weak personality. You will always find reasons why you are not preferred - not because of your competence but due to your looks.

As you continue to feed your conscious mind with certain thoughts, they get registered in your subconscious mind. Soon your involuntary actions will be directed by your subconscious mind. You will start feeling that you do not have much control over your actions and things will happen irrespective of whether you want them to.

But you do have all the control and can use it according to your discretion.

♦ *Say you have the habit of slapping your child when he does not follow your instructions. You may start believing that it is not your problem, but the root of the problem is your child who is not listening, which results in anger and you slap him! In another scenario, you are in your office and have been assigned a task, but you cannot complete it on time. Your boss gets very angry with you and starts using abusive words. How often has it happened that you slap your boss? The possibility is highly unlikely.*

♦ *The only reason you did not slap your boss and controlled your anger is that you know the repercussions! You know that you will lose your job which has led to signal your mind that you need to control yourself in such a situation. Yet, you never control yourself with your child. Why, because you are not giving any signal to your mind that the repercussions will be difficult. So, the entire scenario indicates that while we do feel we are slaves to our habits, in actuality, we have ample power to change our deep-rooted habits, if we have a valid reason.*

How Negative Vibrations Work in Life?

Vibrations can be negative or positive. It depends on the kind of thought process we are creating. In general, we tend to generate negative thoughts. Maybe the surroundings in which we live help us have more negative vibrations! When we say surroundings, we mean the people we meet every day, the food we eat, the social media we follow, the books we read (although rare these days!), the observations we make when travelling by train, bus or metro. All the negative inputs encompass our negative vibration.

In case of a natural calamity like a tsunami, typhoon, earthquake, or incidents of firing in school and government offices and clubs in the US, we support them by sharing money, clothes, blankets, food, flowers and our worries, too! We start sharing negative thoughts with the affected such as "how bad the situation is, how many may have been killed, the numerous houses that have been destroyed, that they have nothing to eat and there is no government support, who will take care of the orphans, what will be their source of livelihood, etc."

Do these people in great difficulty need our negative vibrations? They already have enough of it. What they are presently seeking is a powerful blessing, not worrying thoughts. They want to hear that "everything will be ok soon, God has given them the energy to fight the challenge, and they have enough power to rebound." The greater the problem, the more powerful should be our blessings. This is the best way to support them.

We worry about our children: their studies, careers, coming home late, not getting married, their physical health, etc.

What kind of vibrations will help them do the things we think are good for them? Certainly, the negative will not provide support.

These days there are many incidents of misconduct with girls: young children drink and drive, leading to accidents. Consider your daughter has gone to a party with friends and has not returned home on time. Her mobile phone is not answered. Generally, we start sending negative thoughts her way like what must have happened, is she ok, and the like. What message are we giving her?

In more than 95% of these cases, nothing happens, and the child returns home safely and sound. If she is actually in trouble, what does she requires from us at this point? Do we have the choice of sending different vibrations -- may God bless her, she will be fine, she is stuck somewhere and soon she will be back home -- but what do we do in reality?

If we are to change our thoughts, we need to change our inputs. Let's check our inputs. Whatever goes in will always come back as output. We must radiate the right thoughts. Powerful thoughts like "I am a powerful soul, I can do whatever I want, the world is a beautiful and peaceful place, etc." will help us think positively.

But, why do we think the other way? Once the diet of our minds is right, we can correct any thought we want. As discussed earlier, due to inputs from our surroundings, our minds get affected. When the mind is polluted with negative thoughts, health gets affected. When health is not good, it impacts our relationship with society and social relationships get affected. So, everything gets affected by one or a series of negative inputs.

It's like a mobile phone. Presently, our life revolves around it, which can do everything. Consider if our mobile phone gets infected with a virus, what will happen? The output will not be as we are expecting. There will be errors and slow processing of data. So, for an insignificant tool like a mobile phone (although it is not true now), it should have the right software. Only then, it will work appropriately.

What about our mind, the biggest and most innovative creation of God?

SUMMARY

- **Negative Self-Talk:** From childhood, knowingly and unknowingly, we start creating different types of negative expressions which later turn into negative self-talk (inner chattering). These negative expressions primarily result from our environment, our habits, heredity. Some of the negative expressions are an overreaction, comparison, personalization, absolute language, assumption, expectations, regret.

- **Why do we create Negative Self-Talk:** One of the key reasons for creating negative self-talk is our insecurities towards life. From early childhood, seeds of negativity are fed by our surroundings (Parents, neighbours, Friends, Teachers, Media etc.) to be afraid. It is rightly said that whatever is done repeatedly becomes a part of us (Garbage in – Garbage out).

- **Garbage in:** This is the single most important aspect that designs life. We always think about why things are happening this way or that. Sometimes we think that life is favouring us, but at times we think otherwise. It is important to understand how much garbage was taken in throughout the day and what will happen the next.

- **Garbage out:** When we put the Garbage in throughout the day, it gets processed and Garbage comes out. It is very important to understand that this vicious circle is never-ending. Without realizing it, most of us are completely entangled in it. The more we avoid wrong thoughts from ourselves and others, the better off we will be.

■ **Repetition:** Anything done repeatedly becomes a habit. When we repeatedly give the same signal to our minds like Monday Morning sucks, irrespective of whether that particular Monday is pleasant or not, we will still feel that Monday morning sucks. It is not only we who are getting affected by this repeated self-talk but also the persons surrounding us. When the intention is not right, the possible responses from your subconscious mind will be negative.

■ **How Negative vibrations work in life:** Vibrations can be negative or positive. It depends on the kind of thought process we are creating. In general, we tend to generate negative thoughts. We worry about our children: their studies, careers, coming home late, not getting married, their physical health, etc. What kind of vibrations will help them do the things we think are good for them? Certainly, the negative will not provide support.

THINGS TO PONDER

(a) How often you create Negative Self-Talk?

(b) Does it impact your personal and professional life?

(c) Are you happy with this situation or you are looking for a better option?

CHAPTER

5

Positive Self-Talk

Our happiness or unhappiness in life depends upon our opinions (positive or negative). We create our lives by the statements and questions we say to ourselves and others. Disempowering questions take away our power to act.

Life is nothing more than our opinion of our past, present and future.

Where does our *past* exist?	Only in our minds.
Where does our *present* exist?	Only in our minds.
Where does the *future* exist?	Only in our minds.

*When we **do** meditation, we are fighting to be calm, when we **are in** meditation, we are not fighting, we are flowing.*
— Brahamakumaris

It is important to understand that whenever you want to change any habit, you must first accept that, yes, you do have a challenge in your life. You need to work on it and never fight with yourself. Whenever you try to fight a problem, you generally get even more tired and fatigued. It leads to a situation where you think, "it is difficult to change me" and you decide to continue to be the same. You adjust your lifestyle according to it.

Have you noticed a person swimming in a lake and how much struggle that person may be doing to stay afloat because he/she is trying to fight against the flow, but a *dead body does not drown and floats as it accepts the situation and frees itself!* A leaf just flows in the river as it does not fight. But as we grow in age and stature, we tend to become more rigid and want things to be done our way. In this process, we struggle more. You may have noticed people who work hard day and night but many, never reach their destination.

Positive Thinking

♦ *A person was coming to a new village, relocating, and he was wondering if he would like it there, so he went to the Zen master and asked, "Do you think I will like it in this village? Are the people nice?" The master asked back, "How were the people in the town where you come from?" "They were nasty and greedy; they were angry and lived for cheating and stealing," said the newcomer. "Those are exactly the types of people we have in this village," said the master.*

♦ *Another newcomer to the village visited the master and asked the same question to which the master asked, "How were the people in the town where you come from?" "They were sweet and lived in harmony; they cared for one another and the land;*

they respected each other and were seekers of spirit," he replied. *"Those are exactly the type of people we have in this village,"* said the master.

The quality of our life depends on only two things: the quality of our communication with the world *inside of us* and *outside of us.*

An engineer has a technique and a process for building a bridge or an engine. Like the engineer, your mind also has a technique for governing, controlling, and directing your life.

All experiences, actions, events and circumstances of your life are nothing but reflection and reaction of your thoughts.

If you store the thought, "I generally forget to carry my wallet", you may notice that you often forget to carry it. The subconscious does not ask or question anything. It just performs the task that has been ordered.

You must have heard many times, *"What you sow, so shall you reap"*. This is the work of the subconscious mind. Whatever we do every day becomes our habit. Whatever becomes our habit gets stored in the subconscious mind. Good habits empower the conscious mind to generate positive statements, which when embedded in the subconscious mind create incredible magic in real life.

So, good habits like

> *meditation*
>
> *yoga*
>
> *waking up on time*
>
> *believing in yourself*
>
> *doing positive self-talk*
>
> *seeing the good in others*
>
> *appreciating others*
>
> *loving your spouse/parents/teachers/elders*
>
> *praying to God every day*
>
> *paying your bills on time, etc.*
>
> *It will become a reality when you say...*

result in the subconscious mind generating positive thoughts and the reality gets altered accordingly. When you say...

♦ I am resourceful. You will start finding support from everywhere and you will be amazed.

♦ I always wake up on time. You will find that every morning you wake exactly at the same time that you had planned.

♦ You love your spouse (*only*). You will start finding so many good things that you might not have noticed earlier.

♦ I pay my bills on time. You will find that everything is streamlined and there is no delay.

♦ I pray to the almighty every day. You will find that you have ample time to pray to God and are feeling blessed by doing it.

♦ I am doing meditation every day. You will start finding many people talking about meditation and articles in the newspaper and on social media. You will observe that Meditation seems to be the most popular thing to do.

♦ When you ask empowering questions like, "Why am I able to lose weight?", you will find positive responses like I am focused so I can lose weight, I am good at dieting, I live a healthy life, I work out every day, I enjoy being healthy,

♦ I find everyone around me to be healthy

So, anything repeated again and again becomes a part of us. like

Wow, its Monday morning again

I am raring to go to the office

Let me challenge myself again

Let me see whether I can deliver the best of my potential

As you transform your self-talk from negative to positive, you start waking up all energized and excited even on Monday mornings. You pass on the same vibration to your family. Your child will be kicked up about going to school, meeting friends again, and will be looking forward to learning something new. Your wife will also think that this week will be different from the previous and she will achieve her goals.

As you continue to feed your conscious mind with certain thoughts, they get registered in your subconscious mind. Soon your involuntary actions start directed by your subconscious mind. You will start feeling that you do not have much control over your actions and things will happen irrespective of whether you want them to. But you do have all the control and can use it as per your discretion.

Negative to Positive Thinking

When you are working hard on some ambitious project, someone might ask, "What are the chances of success with this project?" Assume that you respond, "*I am finding it very difficult to complete this project. Although I am hopeful that I will be able to complete the project in time, I am expecting a few roadblocks in the coming weeks.*"

In this conversation, you are giving conflicting communication to the world *inside* yourself. You are giving a message that "there will be roadblocks and you will be finding it difficult to complete the project." You have generated negative thoughts that will continue to hover in your inside world, waiting for something wrong to happen.

Similarly, you are also giving a message to the outside world that "not everything is right and there is a possibility of a delay." So, the vibration that goes out in the universe is that "this guy is facing some problem and expecting roadblocks. So, give him, what he is expecting!" In this way, by talking negative about a situation, you trigger negativity inside and outside your world.

It raises a few pertinent questions, "is it wrong to accept a situation if it is not favourable? Is it not right to share the facts with the outside world? Isn't it fair to tell the inside world that everything is not right and you need to work on it? Are you trying to fool yourselves and others? Are you saying that by not accepting the facts, you can still achieve what you are seeking? Are you not taught in school and college that you must face the facts and fear; only then you can fight it?"

Yes, it is true. The idea is not to avoid anything and not to confront the facts but to find better ways of communicating with your inside and outside world. The idea is to remember the thought, "*what you sow, so shall you reap.*"

Are you following this principle or not?

Are you making sure that what you are feeding into yourselves is of good quality? As you know, and it has been repeated earlier, "garbage in, garbage out."

There can be another way of responding to the same situation. Assume you respond, "*I am sure that I will be completing this project on time. I do have few roadblocks in the way but I am fully prepared and equipped to face them and they will be resolved.*"

Now by changing the words and *still* sharing the facts, what you have achieved is that you have sown seeds of *possibilities*. You create new possibilities when you do things using a different approach when the existing one is not working.

As can be concluded from our study of the subconscious mind (right thoughts and wrong thoughts) that we are *solely* responsible for *our* success/failure. No one can make or break us. Whatever we feed in will leave as output. Like it or not, we have to take responsibility for ourselves. We must trust whatever we are today (rich, poor, educated, intelligent, of high self-esteem, of low self-esteem, popular, etc.) is all because of *our* thought process. Since we have created our destinies, the onus is on us to decide whether we want to carry the legacy forward or change it.

How Positive Thinking Works?

In a Hindu text known as the Rig Veda, Desire is called "the first seed of mind." Everything we do springs forth from a seed of desire.

It is said that the subconscious mind is like a safe deposit bank, where you can store anything and everything, and it will remain there forever. There is no possibility of fraud or siphoning off. One important part of this *bank* is that whatever is stored in it is multiplied multifold. So, you can choose what you want to store in *your* bank. It means your subconscious mind does not believe in comparison and is impersonal. It does not think...

which religion do you belong to

whether the colour of your skin is black, brown or white

are you rich or poor?

Do you belong to a higher or lower caste?

What do others think of you (fool or intelligent)?

It works seamlessly and stores everything forever. It's like a machine that records everything irrespective of the quality of the input data.

You are what your deepest nature is. As your nature, so is your will. As you will, so is your deed. As your deed so is your destiny: Brihadaranyaka Upanishad

These days, we hear a lot about Artificial Intelligence (AI). Do you find any connection between AI and the subconscious mind? If you are active on social media and search for videos related to *Buddhism* on YouTube or Facebook; the next time you search for videos, YouTube/Facebook will recommend videos similar to the ones you watched the previous day (*Buddhism* in this case), even though you did not explicitly ask for it.

Artificial Intelligence gauges that these are videos of interest and presents you with the same ones, not only from the same speaker but also on similar topics spoken by different speakers.

Our subconscious mind works exactly in the same way. If you see a fire near you, whatever is stored in your subconscious mind will come out immediately. Either you run away, or try to douse the fire, or panic and freeze or do whatever is your stored *Sanskars*.*

♦ *A homeowner once remonstrated with a furnace repairman for charging two hundred dollars for fixing his boiler. The mechanic*

---

* Sanskars are dispositions, character or behavioural traits, that exist as default from birth or are prepared and perfected by a person over one's lifetime as imprints on the subconscious: according to various schools of Hindu philosophy.

said, "I charged five cents for the missing bolt and one hundred ninety-nine dollars and ninety-five cents for knowing what was wrong."

◆ *Similarly, your subconscious mind is the master mechanic.*

Let me share my real-life stories where I conquered myself by working on my subconscious mind using positive self-talk.

Story 1

"Do the thing you are afraid to do and the death of fear is certain"
—RALPH WALDO EMERSON

When I was about fifteen years old, I was learning how to swim. One day, accidentally I fell into a pool and went down three times. I can still remember the dark water engulfing my head, and I was gasping for air until the instructor pulled me out at the last moment This experience sank into my subconscious mind, and for years I feared the water. But I wanted to get over this fear. I met an elderly psychologist who said to me, "Go down to the swimming pool, look at the water, and say out loud in strong tones,

I am going to master you

I can dominate you

I have all the abilities to swim and face all the situations

Then go into the water, take lessons, and overcome it." I followed what the psychologist had told me and eventually, I mastered the water. I did not permit the water to master me: I was the master of the water. When I assumed a new attitude of mind, the omnipotent power of the subconscious responded, giving me strength, faith, and confidence to overcome my fear.

Story 2

I had the habit of going to the toilet during the night. The toilet was outside the room. Every time I went, I had that fear someone was following me, standing behind me to hit me. I was always frightened and did not dare look back. I always rushed back to my bedroom after attending nature's call. It continued for many years but I was not happy with my state of mind. I started feeding my mind with thoughts like

> *There is no one behind me*
>
> *I am strong enough to face anyone*
>
> *I am capable of handling any situation*
>
> *I do not believe in such things*

I bombarded my mind with these thoughts for weeks. One night, I was again in the area, having similar thoughts;' but this time, I decided to turn and face the *consequences*! To my utter surprise, there was no one there, only my fear. I conquered myself by instructing my conscious mind that I can do it and I am strong. I realized that whenever I empower my conscious and subconscious mind, things start happening my way.

Story 3

> *"The mind is carried away by the senses. As a boat unanchored can be tossed by the wind"*
>
> —BHAGAVAD GITA VERSE 2.67

In 2019, I participated in a half marathon running competition (21.09 Kms). Before the competition, many questions were running through my mind:

> *Can I finish the race?*
>
> *I have never run more than 15 km at a stretch in my life?*
>
> *Will I be able to finish it in less than 3 hours?*
>
> *What will happen if I have cramps?*
>
> *Will I be able to go to the office the next day?*
>
> *Do I have it in me to complete the race?*
>
> *OH MY GOD, 21 Kms, is it not a crazy thing I am trying to do?*

…and so many other questions. At that time, I had two choices. Either to crumble under the pressure or to overcome the fear of failure. I had faced many failures earlier and after everyone, I always wondered if the "results could have been different had I pursued a little bit more." I realized that failure can be an easy certainty. Let me give my best shot and create some new possibilities. I had experienced many times that as soon as I decided to do something, I started finding support from unexpected places. I decided to follow my dream and go for it. Whenever any negative question used to appear in my mind, I pepped myself up by mentally saying,

- ◆ Yes, I can do it
- ◆ Yes, I have the full capability to do it
- ◆ Yes, I have outstanding stamina
- ◆ Yes, whatever I decide, I have done it

I started visualizing that

- ◆ I am running calmly and smoothly
- ◆ I have completed my race
- ◆ Everyone is greeting me
- ◆ I am fully healthy after completing my race
- ◆ My state of mind is the same as it was in the beginning
- ◆ My competition is with myself
- ◆ I am not competing with anyone but myself
- ◆ If anyone is running faster than me, I am happy for that person
- ◆ If someone is running slower than me, I wish him good luck
- ◆ I am focusing only on myself

By continually throwing positive affirmations at myself, I was able to keep my state of mind positive and healthy. I faced many challenges while running. After I completed ten kilometres, negative thoughts started overpowering me and I questioned: "whether I should continue?" Many times, I thought if I should stop, I cannot bend my knees, my body is not supporting me, my throat is dry, it's too hot.

During that time, I found a group of young runners led by a lady. They called themselves "Bus of 2.45 hours" as their target was to complete the race by that time (Not before, not later!). I started following them. All of a sudden, running became easy as I was with a group of runners who were 100% confident that they would be able to complete the race in 2.45 hours. When you meet likeminded people, your confidence automatically increases.

With their support and guidance, I completed my race exactly in 2.44 hours. It was a very satisfying experience. It gave me the confidence and belief that *"you become what you think."* The reality is "what *you* think and see and certainly NOT what you hear from others." I indeed prepared myself with strenuous exercises for many months for this event. But it is important to supplement it with the *right* thoughts. The power of self-talk enabled me to overcome my inner fears. It motivated me to see the possibility of what I can do. My subconscious mind was giving me the confidence to do it.

When you ask positive questions to yourself, you propel your subconscious mind in that direction.

How to do Positive Self-Talk?

Whatever you talk to yourself, you become like that. When you feed thoughts which raise your morale, you become more confident. When you start talking to yourself that "everything is possible, it is only a matter of seeing it differently, you will start finding ways to do it."

In-tuition

"Without doubt, the mind is unsteady and hard to control but practice and dispassion can restrain it"
—BHAGAVAD GITA VERSE 6.35

To create an aura of positivity, you need to find what you are teaching yourself. It means what *TUITION* you are

feeding *IN* to yourself. Whatever tuition you give to your mind, you become like that. When I talked to myself and said that I can write 600 words every day, I was teaching my mind that I am capable of writing those many words every day. Similarly, when I increased that number to 1000, I felt afraid about whether I would be able to meet that number. When I felt afraid, I would feed into my mind that *"No, it is not possible to do it"*, and my brain responded, it is ok. But, despite being fearful, I then fed into my mind that *"Yes, it is possible to do it"* My brain responded, ok you can do it. So, in *both* cases, the response of my mind was OK. It meant that whatever I taught my mind, it accepted it as is. *Good in-Good out, Garbage in-Garbage out.*

When I fed my mind that I could write 1000 words in a day, different kind of thoughts came to mind.

> *I can do it*
> *I may not be able to do it*
> *I have not done it before*
> *Who has done it before?*
> *I can do it but not every day*

Do I have the ability to write 1000 words every day?

I have never done it before, so I cannot do it

What will happen if I do not write 1000 words?

Who is forcing me to write 1000 words?

There were innumerable thoughts. Interestingly, the majority were negative. So, the tuition that I was giving to my mind was - it is not possible, forget it. Now, instead of feeding negative tuition into my mind, I started feeding it positive tuition like

Yes, I can do it

Yes, I have the potential to do it

I have seen many people who have done it successfully

It is easy to do it

It is achievable

I am strong enough to do it

So, what if I fail I day; I will do it again next day

When the tuition to my mind became positive, I started feeling empowered. When I started feeling empowered, my mind started finding ways to get things done. Automatically, I realized that there are so many ways in which I can consistently write 1000 words every day.

I started finding people in my vicinity who were writing every day

I started finding news and articles in social media where they were teaching how to write every day consistently

I started finding books that I had never stumbled upon earlier guiding me, how to write effectively

So, in-tuition is a powerful tool within us all. It is waiting to be utilized. You need to realize its power. So far, you may be using it unknowingly, mostly in a negative way, sometimes positively too. Now, it is time to use it productively. Life will be full of joy wherever you live, and you will feel like its paradise. Impossible will become "I am possible", and unresolved issues will start giving way to logical solutions.

Impossible ~ I am Possible

> *"A true devotee works independently of the world outside and draws his inspiration, equanimity and ecstasy from the source within himself"*
> —BHAGAVAD GITA VERSE 12.16

If you closely look at the word "impossible" and dissect it. It also means "I'M possible." It means it is possible to do whatever you want. As per a study, by the time a child turns 15, he or she must have heard the word "impossible" more than 16,000 times. When a child at a tender age is fed so much negativity, how can we expect him or her to behave positively when a challenging situation arises? Since the mind has been fed with "not possible" so much, the immediate response will always be negative.

It is important to train your mind in the way *you* want to think. The more you train, the better it will respond. Twenty years back, I had heard the following story which is still relevant today.

♦ *A young boy was living in a village. In his home, a cow gave birth to a calf. His father instructed him to enhance his strength by picking up the calf every day by holding a rope through his teeth. As the calf was young and light in weight, the boy could pick it up easily. His father told him to continue this practice every day. As time passed, both the boy and calf grew in age and weight. Every day, the boy continued his practice religiously. By now, the calf had grown into a full-grown cow.*

♦ *Every year in the village, there was an annual festival where people from nearby villages come to share their talent. This boy was also told to demonstrate his amazing talent. Everyone was astonished that the boy could pick up a cow with his teeth. Once he finished his demonstration, everyone asked, "How could he do it?" The boy replied that it was very easy for him. As he was practising every day, he did not have to exert much effort in picking up the cow with his teeth. He had trained his mind that it is possible to pick up a cow. Since he was practising every day, the thought of not picking up the cow never crossed his mind!*

Whatever way you train your mind, it starts accepting it. If you think it is possible to do something, all the energy from the universe will find a way to do it. You will start seeing newer ways to do the work. Say, you want to learn, how to go fishing?

♦ *You may find it strange, but if you are travelling, your co-passenger will talk to you about ways in which fishing can be done and the purpose of fishing etc.*

- *Suddenly, in your social media like Whatsapp/Instagram, you will start finding messages related to fishing.*

- *You may find a friend talking about his recent experience about fishing*

If you think that something is *not* possible, you will find all the possible ways of how the work cannot be done. Say you want to practice for long-distance cycling but are feeling afraid of starting it.

You may start finding yourself unhealthy

Your doctor may tell you not to do excessive physical activity and much more

Known and unknown people will tell why you should not do it

So, I AM possible or impossible both, are options in your hands. You are the creator of your destiny. You have been empowered with all the energy in the world. It is up to you to tap into that energy. You cannot *entirely* blame your destiny for your success or lack of success in life. You have all the possibilities available to create the destiny you want to have.

Benefits of Positive Self-Talk

"The only questions that really matter are the ones you ask yourself."
—URSULA K. LE GUIN

In your self-talk, when you ask the right questions, you get the right answers. This helps you understand yourself better. When you are open to learning new things and start using self-talk as part of your improvement, it helps you in many ways. Some of the key benefits are:

live life peacefully

Feel stronger, more confident and healthier

More willing to take risks and face challenges; goals look exciting

Experience a deep sense of inner peace

Attract more opportunities

Replace personalization with balanced responsibility

Replace absolute language with a balanced, relative language

Replace assumption with a focus on facts

Replace expectations with curiosity

Replace comparison with cooperation and joy

Replace regret with appreciation

Create positive thoughts

Learn how to listen

Mindfulness

When you start benefitting from positive self-talk, it leads to an improvement in your life at all levels.

Positive Aura

"When we know better, we do better."
—MAYA ANGELOU

Whatever you think, consciously or unconsciously, creates an aura around you. In Hindu mythology, there is white light (*halo*) behind the head of God and the Goddesses (deities).

What does that white light signify? White is the symbol of purity, goodness and peace. The aura of deities denotes purity, innocence, divinity, neutrality and simplicity. When someone has such an aura, what happens? Automatically, people get attracted to it. They find comfort in the vicinity of such a person.

The quality of *your* thoughts makes your aura. When you talk positive to yourself, see positive in others, find goodness in everything, your aura becomes positive (*white*). When you talk negatively to yourself and others, find fault in everything, see problems in every situation, your aura becomes negative (*dark*).

Throughout the day and night, you keep on making, breaking, building, rebuilding, adding, and deleting your aura. You do it consciously and unconsciously by picking up things around you. It is important what you are picking and choosing not to pick.

Whatever you communicate to yourself becomes part of your personality. That creates an aura around you. Whoever comes to touch you will feel the same aura. You must have noticed that when you meet an unknown person, sometimes very quickly you strike up a conversation. Recently I was travelling by train from New Delhi to Gwalior. Besides my seat was a middle-aged gentleman. As soon as I sat, we just started talking and continued for almost 4 hours, till the time I reached my destination; while many times, you find it difficult to even initiate a dialogue. (Remember your last trip by air or train when you spent hours sitting with an unknown person *without* any communication!)

There are many instances when talking to a stranger is very important to get some information or find a solution to a problem. If you have gone to a new city and are looking for a particular address, you will observe that many people cross your path, but you may not be able to muster enough confidence to start a conversation. But there will be *someone* with whom you will find it easy to talk and clarify your query.

Why does this happen? All of them are strangers and they may speak the same language, but you strike up a conversation with only one out of 10. One of the reasons is "the matching of you and the other persons' aura." When it happens, you find it comfortable to initiate a conversation without a hitch.

You must have noticed that sometimes an unknown person helps you without gain or purpose. You may find it strange. You may think it is because of your past karmas or a previous birth (*only if you believe that there is life before and after this!*). Another reason is the kind of aura you create. It gives comfort to others to talk to you without any inhibition.

You must have observed in your school or college day that you were befriended by many. Now, if you look back to find what kind of friends you had during that time, you will see a distinct similarity in your personality and theirs. Why did it happen? The only reason (apart from many others) is the kind of aura that you and your friends were carrying such that you found it easy to talk and become friends.

> *A magnetized piece of steel will lift about twelve times its own weight and if you demagnetize this same piece of steel, it will not even lift a feather*
> —JOSEPH MURPHY

Change from Reaction to Response

> *"His own self must be conquered by the king for all time; then only are his enemies to be conquered"*
> —RISHI VYASA, THE MAHABHARATA, 1000 B.C.

There is a subtle difference between Reaction & Response. When you are reacting, you have little or no control over your action. But when you are responding, you *own* your action.

- ◆ *When you are in the office and get a call from home that your mother has suffered a heart attack, how you will behave?*

- ◆ *When you are with your friends and someone bullies you, what will be your behaviour?*

♦ *You are driving a motorcycle in your lane and suddenly someone crosses you, how you will behave?*

♦ *When you are watching a nail-biting final of any sport (cricket, football) and your home team doesn't win, how you will behave?*

♦ *You are going to a movie with your friends and parking your car. Another car in front of you is moving slowly and delaying you. How you will behave?*

♦ *You are travelling to a different country and after reaching the airport, you realize that your passport is missing. How you will behave?*

♦ *You are on a flight and due to bad weather, the Aeroplane starts shaking. How you will behave?*

♦ *You are at your home and your teenage daughter talks rudely when you ask her to focus on her studies. How you will behave?*

♦ *You are in deep love with your girlfriend but she decides to marry another. When you receive this message, how you will behave?*

There can be umpteen situations like these during the day, where you have a choice of how to behave. But in most cases, you may be *reacting* without using *your* right to *choose* your behaviour.

When I say *react*, I mean replying immediately without thinking. In the above situation where the daughter talks rudely to her father, he immediately shouts back at her or stares with anger. All these actions are without thought, therefore called a reaction.

Many of us generally consider this behaviour to be appropriate and it happens everywhere around us. We feel our actions are justified. If someone suggests a better way, we may not agree with their point of view as whatever is practised by the majority has become our truth.

But there is a different and simpler approach. It is called *response* instead of *reaction*. When you respond, you create a gap to think before acting. When you introduce this gap, you are choosing action within *your* control with no bearing on how others behave under the same situation. Hence, you own your behaviour.

Hence, you own your behaviour. When you *react* instead of *responding*, you lose

♦ Energy

♦ Peace of mind

♦ Relationships with your near and dear ones

♦ Self-control.

When you realize the importance of the damage you are doing, you feel there must be a better way to behave.

Our auto-pilot mode needs to be switched to manual. Our subconscious mind controls all the vital processes of our body and knows the answers to all problems. It multiplies and magnifies whatever we deposit into it like "I am feeling hungry" or "I am feeling sleepy" or "I am looking smart". Since we have behaved in a certain way for years, our subconscious mind activates whenever such situation originates. We lose control of our conscious mind.

Positive Self-Talk helps in designing a new methodology to rewire our subconscious mind. With practice, you can empower your subconscious mind to create an option whenever you are snapping back in any situation. You may not be successful in the beginning, but with consistent practice, whenever you face an unwanted situation, your subconscious will offer an option to choose. You can create your Self-Talk like below.

I have full control over my mind
I say what I want
I behave the way I want
I decide what to say and what not to say

Self-Talk helps us remember that we are the captain of our mind and the master of our fate. You have the capacity to

Choose life!
Choose love!
Choose health!
Choose happiness!

Following are the benefits of living life peacefully in five spheres of life: personal, professional, health, spiritual and relationships.

Personal Life

♦ Relationship with spouse improves

♦ Relationship with children improves

♦ You want to go home on time every day

♦ You look forward to spending quality time with your family

♦ Transparency among family members improves

Professional Life

♦ Relationship with peers improve

♦ Relationship with seniors improve

♦ You do not feel tense on a Monday morning

♦ You do look forward to the weekends!

♦ Work is not a burden but a responsibility

♦ Possibility of promotion and incentives improve

Health

♦ The problem of overweight is controlled

♦ Energy level improves

♦ Diseases like high blood sugar and blood pressure are controlled

♦ Your body remains active throughout the day

♦ The number of medications is reduced

Spiritual Life

♦ Peace of mind is enhanced

♦ You do not deflect much in any situation (good or bad)

♦ Acceptance of a situation increases

♦ Self-awareness improves

♦ Competition shifts from others to the self

Relationships

♦ Your relationship with the self improves

♦ Your relationship with the outside world improves

♦ Value of relationships change from taking benefit to mutual benefits

♦ Acceptability of other improves

SUMMARY

- **Positive Thinking:** The quality of our life depends on only two things: the quality of our communication with the world inside of us and outside of us. Anything repeated, again and again, becomes a part of us. As you continue to feed your conscious mind with certain thoughts, they get registered in your subconscious mind. Soon your involuntary actions will be directed by your subconscious mind.

- **Negative to Positive Thinking:** Only we are responsible for our success/failure. No one can make or break us. Whatever we feed in will leave as output. Like it or not, we have to take responsibility for ourselves. By changing the words and still sharing the facts, we can sow seeds of possibilities.

- **How Positive Thinking Works:** The subconscious mind is like a blank slate, where you can store anything and everything, and it will remain there forever. Whenever you empower your conscious and subconscious mind, things start happening your way. By continually throwing positive affirmations at yourself, you can keep your state of mind positive and healthy.

- **How to do Positive Self-Talk:** To create an aura of positivity, you need to find what you are teaching yourself. Whatever tuition you give to your mind, you become like that. When the tuition to your mind becomes positive, you start feeling empowered. You are the creator of your destiny. You have been empowered with all the energy in the world. It is up to you to tap into that energy.

■ **Benefits of Positive Self-Talk:** Whatever you think, consciously or unconsciously, creates an aura around you. The quality of your thoughts makes your aura. When you talk positive to yourself, see positive in others, find goodness in everything, your aura becomes positive. Some of the benefits of positive self-talk include healthy: personal life, professional life, spiritual life and relationships.

THINGS TO PONDER

(a) Think about positive talk self-talk that you did and the benefits you got from it.

(b) Think about your successes that you have got so far from positive thinking

(c) Can you think about the people around you who are successful and happy? What qualities they must be carrying with themselves?

CHAPTER

6

Side Impact of Positive Self-Talk!

If a ladder is not leaning against the RIGHT wall, every step we take just gets us to the wrong place faster
— STEPHAN R COVEY

While self-talk is a wonderful experience, it is also important to understand what we are seeking through it. Sometimes through positive self-talk, we try to achieve *half-truths*, which work well for some time, but after a while, we find that we have arrived at a place we never wanted to reach!

Say you are preparing for a job interview. The positive self-talk could be on the line that ensures things happen the way *you* want them to be.

I will start at home on time.

I will reach the interview venue on time.

I will be the first person to be interviewed.

The interviewer will compliment me for my sharp and classy dress.

The interviewer will be impressed by my qualification and certificate.

The interviewer will start the interview by asking the question, "tell something about yourself".

Since I have prepared myself so well, I will start from my school days and share everything precisely in two minutes.

The interview will end on a positive note.

They will ask me to wait for 30 minutes but in 20, they will call me and share the good news that I have been selected. WOW.

Now, this is wonderful positive self-talk you can engage in continually and train your mind to visualize every statement that you practised during self-talk. The only anomaly in this positive self-talk is that you are not only trying to control *your* future but also predicting the actions of another person, over whom you do not have any control.

You do have control over your qualifications and achievements, choice of dress, etc. but ask yourself:

Do I have control over traffic?

Do I have control over the other person's perception of my dress?

Do I have control on the slot at which I'll be called for the interview?

Do I have control over the sequence and type of questions that will be asked?

Do I have control over the decisions of another person?

What if: you get stuck in traffic or the office elevator and arrive late, all angry and agitated. Then the types of questions the interviewer chooses are entirely other than your expectations and you will feel unprepared.

When the result comes contrary to the positive self-talk, you get demotivated and conclude that positive self-talk is bullshit and does not work.

When all these unexpected events happen, what do you think happens to your morale? How will you perform and respond if the result is not in your favour?

♦ *I will not be in my rhythm*

♦ *I will be surprised by the questions and try to stick to my sequence of questions and prepared answers, which will eventually fall flat*

♦ *In case the result is not in my favour, I will stop believing in positive self-talk as well as myself*

♦ *Rather than getting ready to challenge me for the next interview, I will start finding faults in my capability*

Now, think about positive self-talk in a different scenario.

Assume you get selected for the job. Your belief in positive self-talk will increase. You will feel that this is the right path to follow. You can control *others* by doing positive self-talk. Other persons and situations will tend to change based on your talk. You can duplicate this learning in upcoming projects and you will continue to practice it for different scenarios.

♦ *How your boss will behave with you?*

♦ *How you will crack a new deal for your business?*

◆ *How you will impress your spouse?*

◆ *How will you attain high grades on examinations?*

The only challenge in this positive self-talk is that we are trying to control *another* person and situation. We start writing the *script* for the other person, who is not in our control. Sometimes we may be successful, but what will be the cost of our success? It is very important to understand if we are looking for long-term sustenance.

Let me share experience and how I realized the pitfall of this self-talk.

◆ *In 2002, I was assigned a task to be completed within one year. As per my learning at that time, I started visualizing the picture one year later, the project completed successfully and everyone clapping for me and appreciating my efforts. Every day I used to do the self-talk that everyone is supporting me, whatever the challenges, they are converting in my favour. With this visualization, I continued to work with the best of my energy. Fortunately, I was successful in my planning and whatever I visualized happened.*

This empowered me to continue with the theory of positive self-talk and visualization. I thought that I was on the right track. With practice, I achieved success in many upcoming projects.

A few years later in 2011, I again came across an ambitious project. I copied my previous experience and continued with self-talk and visualization. I was very sure that this time, too, people would behave in the way I wanted, that situations would turn positive. But this time, the result was not in my favour. I was hugely disappointed.

Moreover, the stress of success affected my health. The problem was that I was trying to control the situation rather than *myself*. Since I had been successful for many years, I could not comprehend why I was not successful this time? It took me a couple of years to resolve the mystery. I found that I was not only predicting my behaviour but was also dictating how others would behave—the way I wanted!

> *You have the right to work, but never to the fruit of work. You should never engage in action for the sake of reward nor should you long for inaction*
> —BHAGAVAD GITA

No one has control over another person's behaviour and attitude. It may be a coincidence that the other person and situation behave the way you want, but it is temporary. When you start believing that the other person will follow your instruction, you are becoming a judge of *their* destiny.

The only person or situation you can control is *you*. During the journey, while doing self-talk and visualization, you need only focus on *your* efforts and behaviour. At the end of the project, irrespective of the result, you will remain in control and healthy. If the result is in your favour, it is wonderful; if not, *you will remain in a positive mental state and be ready to face challenges again.*

> *A person can rise through the efforts of his own mind or draw himself down in the same manner because each person is his own friend or enemy*
> —BHAGAVAD GITA

♦ *If you are planning to conduct an annual appraisal of your colleagues, you prepare the type of questions and behaviour you want to portray. While conditioning your mind, you start creating images of your colleagues, how they will respond to your intricate queries. You also assume that when you appreciate and propose a high increment, your colleague will be flabbergasted and appreciate you more.*

♦ *Sometimes, we create a negative picture such that when we are discussing a serious topic with a peer, we start imagining how they might not take our discussion seriously, leading to strong arguments.*

In both situations, you are not only assuming your behaviour but also dictating the behaviour of another person as well. If it does not work out your way, it will lead to a lot of disenchantment. Even without real-time experience, you tend to believe that things will happen in a particular fashion or you get tense. If you are thinking of good results, you become happy without any reason. So, even before the real-life situation, our *present* gets affected by predicting our *future,* which is not in our hands.

What is the solution? As stated above in the epic scripture, Bhagavad Gita, we are the controller of our destiny and the destroyer too. We have immense power within to do whatever we want. It can be with a positive spirit like what Mahatma Gandhi or Nelson Mandela did for the community or with a negative spirit like Adolf Hitler.

SUMMARY

- **Positive Self-Talk** is wonderful, provided we are sure, how we are practising it. When used correctly, it will produce extraordinary results. If not utilized appropriately, we may get demotivated and start disbelieving it.

THINGS TO PONDER

(a) Can you think about any incident where positive self-talk did not work for you?

(b) What were the possible reasons?

CHAPTER

7

Conclusion

As you are on the verge of completing this book, it is very important to retrospect and crystallize **the key takeaways for you.**

What is Self-Talk

The inner chatter that continues throughout day and night. It can be done consciously but the majority of the time it happens unconsciously. This inner chatter can be positive or negative. If positive, it makes us cheerful, confident and supportive. If negative, it results in the generation of self-defeating thoughts. We often talk to ourselves in statements like "I can't do anything right" or "I'm a complete failure."

Difference between Negative and Positive Self-Talk

Positive Self-Talk	Negative Self-Talk
Motivates you to do anything	Demotivates you to try anything new
Helps in challenging the present state	Hinders you from doing anything creative
Empowers you to move to the next level	Disempowers you when it comes to trying anything new
Helps you see everything positively	Pushes you to find faults in every situation
Guides you to the path of success	Drives you to remain wherever you are
Dilutes the pessimism inside you	Adds to the pessimism inside you

Difference between Conscious and Subconscious Mind

Conscious Mind	Subconscious Mind
Active mind	Reactive mind
Takes decision-based on the actual situation	Takes a decision based on the data stored inside it
Can change our decision making immediately	Stops us from making any change easily

Benefits of Positive Self-Talk

◆ Keeps you healthy.

◆ Keeps you vibrant.

◆ Keeps you active.

◆ Keeps you alive.

- Keeps you joyful.

- Makes life simpler & happier.

- Challenges you to try new things.

- Keeps you grounded.

- Makes your inner chatter positive.

- Helps you to see positives even in an adverse situation.

- Helps you to be optimistic in every situation.

How to Incorporate Positive Self-Talk?

(a) **Identify Thoughts & Benefits you are seeking**

- do you want to feel good about yourself?

- do you want to feel empowered about yourself?

- do you want to feel strong & fully charged (not drained) when you reach home in the evening?

- do you want to remain in a positive state of mind?

- do you want to have good thoughts about your future?

- do you want to feel secure about your career?

(b) **Implement it**

Once you are clear about your objectives for Self-Talk, it is important to start working on it. You do charge your mobile in the morning so that it remains charged throughout the day. Similarly, it is important to charge *yourselves* fully so that you can remain emotionally strong till the evening. If the mobile battery drains down, it is easy to charge, but for human beings, it takes more effort. So, it is equally important to keep yourselves charged. There are several ways to feed your mind. Some of them include

♦ Meditation

♦ Listening to positive self-talk (you can create your own self-talk or you can listen to prerecorded self-talk on YouTube)

♦ Listening to soulful music while doing yoga/ morning walk

♦ Avoid listening to the news in the morning

♦ Not reading newspaper in the morning

♦ Not checking social media updates in the morning on Facebook/Twitter/Instagram etc

(c) **Check the effectiveness**

At times if you overuse the mobile, you do need to charge it in the afternoon or evening, sometimes you carry a power bank with yourself. In case you are not receiving updates on social media, you also regularly check whether signals are coming or not. Sometimes you use 2 mobiles or double SIM mobile as a backup. Similarly, for ensuring positive state of mind, it is important to verify your state of mind (what signals your mind is giving or how strong are the signals or whether you are fully charged or getting drained out). You can have

♦ hourly alarm to check your status

♦ quick 1-minute positive self-talk to pep up yourselves

♦ during breaks, you can listen to powerful thoughts for at least 2 to 5 minutes

♦ you can devise any other method which suits you.

(d) Continue and reap its benefits

In your job or business, you do review your performance daily, weekly, monthly and yearly. Similarly, to review your state of mind, it is pertinent to have a daily review before going to bed. The intent is to check what you have achieved and where you need to improve. Before sleeping, it will be wonderful if you read a self-help book or listen to powerful thoughts so that while sleeping positive thoughts can ingrain in your subconscious mind. You may also feel that during the day, you have failed miserably but it is fine, you can try the next day again. Another question is "for how long you need to review your performance?" The simple answer is *"till the day you want to feel empowered and strong."*

Possible Challenges

♦ You may not like the idea of monitoring yourself.

♦ You always want to be a free bird!

♦ You may not want anyone including yourselves to change yourself.

♦ You always have very high thoughts about yourselves.

♦ You may always think that these things (Self-Talk) is for others and not for me.

♦ You may think that you are fully competent to manage yourselves.

- You may have seen many failed examples wherein someone had tried doing differently but failed.

- You do not want to face failure.

- Rather than thinking "what if it works", You have a stronger feeling "what if it does not work?"

- You may think that "If I have managed myself in this way so far and I am reasonably successful, why should I try something new?"

- Another thought could be "if others are not doing, why should I?"

- If they are managing, I can also manage.

It is very strange; we all remember one bad example and keep repeating it with everyone but do not talk about others who have been successful in changing themselves.

What if, you don't Implement?

- You will continue to have negative thoughts
- Your mood will swing automatically
- Your subconscious mind will decide what you need to do
- You will continue to have self-doubt
- You will continue to feed Garbage in and wonder why Garbage is coming out
- You will continue to over-react
- You will continue to expect from others and when not received, will feel depressed

What Next after this?

♦ Sustain this practice and see the benefits. You have taken years to change (*good to bad*) yourselves to the present state. It will take some time to reverse the process.

♦ Once you feel successful, do share it with others. Continue with the practice and it will open new doors for you, which you had never expected.

THINGS TO PONDER

(a) What did I learn from this book?

(b) What are the key takeaways?

(c) How I am going to implement these new learnings?

(d) What do I need to do to make it sustainable?

ABOUT THE AUTHOR

Bhavya Mangla is a Quality Management System professional with 28 years of experience in System auditing, Automotive sector, Steel sector and packaging sector. By qualification, he is an Industrial Engineer who did his MBA in Marketing Management.

He is a long-distance runner who has participated in many half marathons. Learning public speaking skill is his passion which has resulted in him being part of Toastmasters for over 6 years. After learning life skills by exposing himself to multi-level marketing companies, the process of knowing himself started. This paved the way for his spiritual journey.

Although reticent in political activities around the country, he has been able to remain an impartial thinker, who can see both sides of the stories with equanimity and understanding.